Emerging from the Chrysalis

Emerging from the Chrysalis

Studies in Rituals
of Women's
Initiation

Bruce Lincoln

Harvard University Press
Cambridge, Massachusetts
and
London, England
1981

To my parents,
grandparents,
and children

Library of Congress Cataloging in Publication Data
Lincoln, Bruce.
  Emerging from the chrysalis.

  Bibliography: p.
  Includes index.
  1. Puberty rites. 2. Women (in religion,
folklore, etc.) 3. Rites and ceremonies.
I. Title.
GN483.3.L56   392'.14   80-24189
ISBN 0-674-24840-6

Foreword
by Laura Bohannan

The issues raised in *Emerging from the Chrysalis* are wider than the topic suggests.

Professor Lincoln makes his argument through the medium of five case studies: the Tiyyar of India, the Navajo of the American Southwest, the Tiv of Nigeria, the Tukuna of Brazil, and the Mysteries of Eleusis in ancient Greece as revealed in the myth of Persephone. In terms of geographic, economic, and social variation, the examples are indeed well chosen.

In one more regard these case studies must engage our attention. Three—Tiyyar, Navajo, Tukuna—are unequivocally female initiation rites. Here Lincoln is free to develop conclusions without any question as to the relevance of the data. The other two pose serious problems of treatment and are therefore at once the least satisfying ethnographically and yet the most significant for general theory.

In the first case, that of the Persephone myth and the eternal Mysteries of Eleusis, the question is one we all face. When the culture is no longer a living one, what of relevance can be found, given the absence of liturgical manuals, in historical and literary sources? This is not only the historian's or the classicist's question. In a very similar vein are the anthropological fieldworker's problems in evaluating the pertinent ethnographies of a past generation: Had the culture studied changed in those past years? Or had its previous recorder been a purblind fool? As the time distance increases, the problem becomes more acute. The way in which Lincoln deals with this situation deserves study and congratulation. His separation of data and deduc-

tion, of myth and mystery, accompanied as it is by their synthesis, is
masterly.

The second case, that of the Tiv, raises a different question. What
justification does one have for positing ritual in those areas in which
the people themselves deny that ritual exists—especially when they
admit ritual in other areas? Certainly this problem vexed both Paul
Bohannan and me during and after our years among the Tiv. We de-
cided that the last word lies with the people. Lincoln takes the other
horn of the dilemma.

If one grants the existence of unconscious ritual, Lincoln's Tiv argument is a brilliant one. It concerns the scarification of women's
stomachs, especially in its first patterning. Lincoln suggests that the
circles around the navel represent the age set and give generational
reference; the lines, representing the *nongo,* give genealogical depth.

But such an interpretation fails to match the data. The *nongo* is indeed graphically shown by the Tiv with a line; it is, however, the lineage as a cross-section in time, by definition without depth. The age
set (*kwav*) has no graphic representation among the Tiv. The image of
the ever-expanding circles is not that of ethnography but that of an
ethnographer. So seen, Lincoln's conclusions are inapplicable.

However, the Tiv do represent the lineage cross-section by a line.
They do graphically represent the *tar,* or land, by a circle, and the *tar*
does connote genealogical time. Thus, we can come by another route
to Lincoln's own conclusions, differently derived: the circles, symbo-
lizing genealogical depth and affiliation, are pierced by lines signifying the living generational moment. Furthermore, such an association
of the circle with the *tar* gives greater meaning to the postulated association of female scarification with the *Imborivungu,* a prime symbol of
the *tar.* It also allows us to include without difficulty the presence of
the same scar patterns on the backs of some young men, those who
find them handsome.

The introduction of these alternate interpretations might deserve
footnote treatment, did they not illustrate the difficulty of dealing
with unconscious ritual. Direct testimony having dropped the reins,
the commentator can take the bit between his teeth. Many of us are
too prudent or too cowardly to venture onto such uncertain ground.
Some of us think it wrong to do so. Yet avoidance of the issue is no
answer to the problem. Again, Lincoln shows us how fruitful such an
attempt may be.

The main themes in the discussion of women's ritual initiation
stress the imposition of culture upon nature, of cosmos upon chaos;
the complementary union of opposites resulting in an entity greater
than its components; and the association of female fertility with

plenty. The apparent exception to this rule demonstrates it. The Tu-kuna, who are primarily hunters and fishers, ritually stress the limita-tion of female fertility; this limitation on birthrate is clearly asso-ciated with the maintenance of a favorable ecology (too many people = too little game = dearth for man and beast). All these points give us important insights into the nature of ritual as well as into the nature of women's initiation.

Some of the disciplines of the argument—for example, the Aristo-telian—are probably uncomfortable for an anthropologist, for good but not wholly complimentary reason. Many disciplines contribute to anthropology, especially in the field of theory. Jurisprudents and an-thropologists have tilted for decades: Is Roman law applicable to those who know nothing of Rome? Should the principles of law be derived from the jural practices of each culture and society? The de-bates of anthropologists over economics continue. First stated in terms of classical economics, and now in the formulations of Marxists, the attacks on substantive economy as given by the ethnographer and historian still flourish. The religious view, even when carried to the point of extreme theology, is of equal importance (Lincoln is not an anthropologist but a historian of religions).

The very importance of such contributions tends to hide the fact that none can be swallowed whole by anthropology any more than anthropology, as a whole, can be accepted without predigestion. The exchange is, however, asymmetrical. Other disciplines look to anthro-pology for data (which are often misunderstood through the lack of informing theory). Law, religion, economics, psychology, and so forth offer anthropology classifications and sometimes theory (often misun-derstood from a failure to appreciate the nature of the relevant data). The process, nonetheless, remains of extreme value.

Anthropology is inevitably the poorer when it attempts to be pure. It always needs, and should heed, such voices as Bruce Lincoln's.

Preface

It is difficult to say just when and where a book has its beginnings. To the best of my memory, this one began in the winter of 1973, when I first happened upon a photo of a fully scarified Tiv woman. The pattern of scars she wore with such evident pride was so strange, so complex, and so beautiful that it was unlike anything I had ever encountered before, and I felt driven to learn more about it. Turning to the standard ethnographic literature on the Tiv, I read statements to the effect that the pattern had no significance whatever, but was merely cosmetic or aesthetic in function—statements made by male colonial authorities and male anthropologists on the basis of information furnished them primarily by male informants. This further piqued my curiosity, for everything about the pattern and the way in which it was applied indicated to me that it contained some deeper meaning. Ultimately, I think I was able to uncover that deeper meaning—to demonstrate how the pattern of scars served to orient each Tiv woman within cosmic history, revealing to her her place as descendant of her ancestors and forebear of future generations, guarantor of the continuity of her lineage and her people. The result was my first publication: "The Religious Significance of Women's Scarification among the Tiv," a much abbreviated version of Chapter 4 of this volume.

That article, however, addressed only the narrow problem of what the haunting pattern of scars meant. Beyond that, there lay any number of questions far broader and more vexing. What is a ritual? Could the cursory application of scars among the Tiv be regarded as one? How did this action correspond to ceremonies performed for women in other cultures, and how do those correspond to those performed for men? Do women have a separate ritual and religious life? How does this relate to their separate social, economic, and political life? Is the human species really one, or are the lives of men and women so different that they must be treated separately? The Tiv materials led legitimately to all these issues, and all of them I managed to avoid.

Nevertheless, the Tiv study was particularly rewarding for me in a number of ways. It was a powerful confrontation with dual otherness: *an*other culture, incalculably different from mine, and *the* other gender, perhaps no less different from mine, however similar I had previously assumed it to be. Such a confrontation with otherness is always of value: it reminds one of the relativity and idiosyncrasy of one's own situation in time, body, and space; it sensitizes one to the enormous range of behaviors and ideas that are contained within humanity; and when one does recognize genuine similarities between one's own world and that of another, it often comes with the force of a revelation from on high. In retrospect, I find that my perception of time and of my position within my lineages—familial and academic—has been altered by my confrontation with the scars on Tiv women.

Heir to the ancestors, progenitor of future generations, a pivot in the passage of time: such is the position of all people, regardless of culture or sex. The point was brought home to me again during the writing of this book. On March 8, 1977, three days after my thirtieth birthday, my grandfather, Frank William Lincoln, died—a man of infinite gentleness and enormous strength, of adamant conviction and eternal openmindedness, perhaps the sweetest radical that has ever lived. On December 17, 1977, my first children, Rebecca Anne Lincoln and Martha Louise Lincoln, were born. They have lain, sat, stood, crawled, and walked beside me as I prepared the final chapters of this book.

Ironically, I learned of an unreported rite of women's initiation when my family gathered to pay final homage to my grandfather. I was moved by the story, and I set it down here. In 1919, in Arden, Delaware, a girl seven years of age was about to lose her first tooth. She and her parents had watched with great interest as the tooth gradually became looser, and when it seemed just about ready to go, a ceremony was arranged. All the children of the neighborhood were assembled at the family house, which was marked by projecting beams in the construction of the roof. Over the central beam, a heavy rope had been thrown, one end of which was tied to a large pair of iron ice tongs. A silk thread was tied to one of the pincers on the tongs, and the free end of this thread was fastened to the loose tooth. Once this apparatus was all in place, the children who had gathered grabbed hold of the rope. To cries of "heave-ho," they rhythmically pulled until the tooth came free and was carried aloft by the silken thread. Immediately, the girl was whisked to a wagon painted and decorated to look like an ambulance. There enthroned, she was led triumphantly through town, surrounded by her cheering playmates. The initiand in this ritual was my aunt, Elsie Lincoln Rosner; the inventor and high priest of the ceremony, my grandfather.

There are many people to thank and many debts to acknowledge. First and foremost, I want to express my gratitude to my wife, Louise Lincoln, who has gone over countless outlines, rough sketches, drafts, revisions, and final manuscripts, making invaluable suggestions at every step of the way. Her thoughts and comments pervade all of the book, and her astute criticism has forced me to reassess my thinking on a number of crucial points. If I, as a man, show any understanding of women's lives—and I'm not at all sure that I do—it is no doubt due to Louise's influence. Where I am insensitive or blind, it is almost certainly in spite of her best attempts.

Invaluable suggestions were also made by Kees Bolle, John Carman, Arthur Hinrichs, Judith Modell, Wendy Doniger O'Flaherty, and Benjamin Ray, all of whom were good enough to read portions of my manuscript in earlier stages. Their comments were extremely helpful and kept me from serious blunders in many instances; what errors remain are my responsibility alone.

I would like to thank the following for permission to make use of various figures that appear within the text: the Peabody Museum of Archaeology and Ethnology for Figure 5; the University of Arizona Press for Figure 6; Life Picture Service for Figure 7; the Honorable Editor of *Man* for Figure 11, 12, 15, and 16; Oxford University Press for Figure 14; the editors of *Paideuma* for Figures 18 and 21; Princeton University Press for Figures 25, 26, and 29; Routledge and Kegan Paul for Figure 26; the Metropolitan Museum of Art for Figure 27; and the Cambridge University Press for Figure 28. I would also like to thank the editors of *Paideuma* for permission to make use of material from my article "Women's Initiation among the Navaho: Myth, Rite, and Meaning" (*Paideuma* 23 [1977]:255–263) in Chapter 3; the International African Institute for use of material from "The Religious Significance of Women's Scarification among the Tiv" (*Africa* 45 [1975]:316–326) in Chapter 4; and the President and Fellows of Harvard College for use of material from "The Rape of Persephone: A Greek Scenario of Women's Initiation" (*Harvard Theological Review* 72 [1979]:223–235) in Chapter 6.

Special thanks also go to Ardis Ronnie, who tirelessly and uncom-

plainingly typed the manuscript, and to William O. Miles, who prepared and helped design the illustrations. I am particularly grateful
to the University of Minnesota for two timely grants that enabled me
to complete my research and writing.

Finally, I am grateful to my teachers, particularly Mircea Eliade,
Charles Long, and Peter Slater, and to my students, especially those
in my seminars on "Interpretation of Ritual" and "Rituals of Initiation." In all things, we are between ancestors and descendants.

Contents

Illustrations

1

Introduction

I have some serious reservations about undertaking a study of women's rites of initiation, and perhaps it is best to air them at the outset. Propitiated, they may be robbed of some of their power; unacknowledged, they can only haunt the attempt that follows. To begin, I am not at all certain that any man genuinely understands the lives of women, or that it is possible for one to do so. Similarly, I have doubts that a member of one culture can ever acquire more than a superficial understanding of the important aspects of another culture, let alone those of several other cultures, as I have tried to do here. I am also concerned about whether valid conclusions can be drawn from this kind of comparative research, or whether one can merely hope to assemble a diverting collection of strange customs from faraway lands. There is, however, at least one issue on which I am certain, and that is that despite recent strides forward,[1] to date no one has succeeded in understanding in any real depth what ritual is, does, or means.

It is this last point that concerns me most. When all is said and done, the primary goal of my research is not a better understanding of the lives of women in various cultures, however desirable that might be. As a man and as a historian or religions, I am not really qualified to take up a question that is fundamentally social, psychological, and—above all—political and economic in nature. There are others far more capable of writing on what women's rituals have to tell us about women, and I can only hope that my data are of use and of interest to them in that endeavor. The question I will focus on is a different one, and one that may strike many as a good deal less interesting and worthwhile: What can women's rituals tell us about ritual?

1

Such a judgment, however, seems to me unwarranted, for few elements in human culture are as rich, as varied, or as enduring as ritual. It is evident in the remains of the earliest dwellings of paleolithic man, and depending on definition it may also be observed in the behavior of animals, which would date its origin anterior to the appearance of man.[2] In virtually all cultures, it attends the great turning points of life—with regard to the individual (birth, puberty, marriage, death) and with regard to society as a whole (the rise and fall of governments, the turning of the seasons, the beginning of the new year). Rituals provide the most solemn moments of existence, and also the most festive and raucous. People's actions are most structured, habitual, and bound by rules in the course of ritual, yet conversely it is then that people are most free, being liberated from the tedium and drudgery of everyday life. Great civilizations can devote the labor of their best minds over a period of centuries to the development of ritual, as was the case with the Vedic sacrifice and the Catholic liturgy, while other rites no less beautiful or deep can spring up almost spontaneously and effortlessly.[3]

The existence of ritual is a constant in human society, a true culture universal. It is present in the earliest communities of which we have knowledge, and it persists in the most supposedly secular of environments, although it may take some curious forms in the latter. Thus, a ritual structure has been recognized in such common events as going to a movie, greeting a friend, or writing a footnote, not to mention more obvious examples like athletic contests, psychoanalytic practice, or political campaigns.[4] This is not just to say that these acts are habitual, although repetition is undoubtedly a hallmark of the rite, but also that they are set apart from mundane existence, governed by strict rules of procedure, marked by an elaborate symbolism, and invested with a significance that transcends their strictly physical importance.

Given these points, there has been no shortage of research on the topic of ritual, and theories regarding its nature abound. There are theories of ritual as communication,[5] as play,[6] as the repetition of primordial events;[7] as theater,[8] the dramatization of social relations,[9] and the cultic enactment of myths;[10] as "a routine of external forms,"[11] "the regulated symbolic expressions of certain sentiments,"[12] and the effervescence that shatters the quietude of the everyday world.[13] Still further, there are theories of ritual as the canalization of aggression,[14] as a regulating mechanism for the local economy and ecology,[15] as a form of compulsion neurosis,[16] as the means of mediating between sacred and profane,[17] and of annihilating historical time.[18] These and countless other interpretations of ritual have been offered, and in each there is some truth. The phenomenon is so varied and so complex that in all likelihood there is no single definition that will encompass it, and additional theories still may be necessary to explain some facet or other of any given ceremony.

Although a thorough review of the literature might be instructive and interesting, I am going to resist the temptation (or better yet, the habit) of offering one at this juncture. My intention is not to discuss theories of ritual, but to discuss rituals themselves. All too often scholars—even those such as anthropologists, orientalists, or historians of religions, whose stated goal is to understand the minds of people quite different from themselves—end up writing lengthy volumes in which they discuss nothing but other scholars, that is, those who are most like themselves in every way.[19]

One fact that I might briefly mention regarding the literature on ritual, however, is the relatively small number of rites that have contributed significantly to the formation of current theory. In general, sacrifice has been the most studied rite, Hebraic sacrifice and Vedic sacrifice having been particularly influential, along with Australian totemic sacrifice and that of Diana's priest at Nemi.[20] New Year's ceremonies, particularly the Babylonian Akitu festival, have also been the starting point for numerous scholars, as have the men's initiation ceremonies of the Australian aborigines.[21]

But beyond these few categories—sacrifice, new year, male initiation—there are innumerable rites that have been reported, often abundantly so, but that have not been utilized sufficiently in the formation of general models of ritual. Sacred dances are countless, well documented, and of tremendous importance, but beyond a few outdated volumes almost nothing has been written about them at a theoretical level.[22] Only recently have works appeared on healing ritual,[23] pilgrimage,[24] or divination,[25] and there is still virtually nothing on such rites as oath-taking, the parade, preliminaries to artistic creation, sanctuary, criminal execution, and many more. It is thus one goal of this book simply to expand the base of data from which we draw our generalizations about ritual. For although women's initiation is, in fact, practiced by more societies than is men's initiation, it has been studied much less frequently.[26] And if the women's rites differ significantly from their more studied male counterparts, it may be that our notions of what ritual is and does are in serious need of reassessment.[27]

Twin dangers attend any study of ritual, however. On the one hand lies superficiality, the more dangerous of the two. Glib multiplication of examples bearing a casual resemblance to one another without careful attention to detail and respect for the integrity of the cultures in which the rites are found not only can prove nothing, but will probably lead to misleading results, as was true in so many pioneer works in anthropology and history of religions. On the other hand, the reaction against the excesses of Tylor, Frazer, Wilhelm Schmidt, and others has produced a Scylla to match the Charybdis of superficiality: provincialism. Thus, there are those who decry the possibility of generalization at all, and others who would build general theories on a single well-chosen example, a dubious method at best.

I have tried to steer between these two dangers by working from a few select case studies, five to be exact, although there were many other possible examples I considered using at one point or another. Ultimately, I selected rituals drawn from South India, the American Southwest, West Africa, the Northwest Amazon, and ancient Greece. In making these selections, I was guided by two prime considerations. First, it was necessary that there be sufficient data available for meaningful analysis, which meant that the rite itself had to be reported in minute detail, and that there be solid, dependable ethnographies for the culture in which the rite was performed. All too often this simple test could not be met, and many promising examples had to be rejected. Of those that remained, I chose the five treated here on the basis of their variety, both in terms of geographical distribution and of general morphology. To note but one variable, they range from the most pacific of ceremonies to the most convulsive, from those in which the initiand figures as recipient of infinite care and attention to those in which she is victim of violence and rape. For simplicity's sake, the case studies have been organized along this spectrum, but other schemes of organization might have served equally well.

There are two types of example which I had originally hoped to include, but ultimately rejected for differing reasons. The first is that form of initiation which involves clitoridectomy or other genital surgery as its culminating act. At least two different sets of meaning can be attached to this practice, both of which have been well articulated elsewhere and may thus be briefly summarized. On the one hand, cultures that preserve myths in which primordial perfection is embodied in the figures of androgynous ancestors frequently practice clitoridectomy and circumcision together, as the means of removing children from a state of androgyny and introducing them into sexuated adult existence. The prepuce thus is seen to represent the female element in boys, and the clitoris, the male element in girls.[28] Among other peoples, however, where female genital surgery such as infibulation is practiced without a corresponding operation on males, these operations are set within an overriding code of honor, and function to preserve, dramatize, or even recreate a woman's virginity, as for instance in those cultures where genital surgery is performed after the birth of every child.[29]

If these examples have been so well reported as to make inclusion here superfluous, the state of affairs is not nearly so happy in the case of women's initiations from Oceania. To my regret, I have not been able to locate an example here for which there is sufficient information accessible to permit thorough study.[30] Perhaps female initiation is not practiced so extensively in this region as in other areas of the globe—South America and West Africa, for instance—or perhaps it just has not been reported so well. Australia, where much superb fieldwork has been done for almost a century, offers several possible examples, but given the undue weight that has been placed on Australian male initiation ceremonies in the past, I was reluctant to repeat this error on the female side of things.[31]

One could legitimately ask whether the five case studies presented here really constitute sufficient data for generalization, or whether the conclusions I reach in Chapter 7 might be completely different had I started with five other examples. There is no easy answer to such a question. As a general principle of method, I think it is preferable to argue from a few clear and penetrating examples subjected to thorough analysis than to multiply examples that are, perforce, presented in a more superficial fashion. On the strength of the examples I have examined but not included here, I suspect that they would not have led to different conclusions, only richer ones. Clearly, however, much work remains to be done.

At a quite different level from that of conclusions, generalizations, and theoretical formulations, it is my hope that each of the five case studies can stand on its own as an independent analysis of one specific ritual. The five rituals are strikingly different in their details and one would be hard pressed to see any sort of universal meaning, structure, or symbolism at work in them. Rather, they represent the different ways in which different cultures have responded to the same situation: the moment at which a girl becomes a woman. Accordingly, I have avoided any use of comparative method within the case studies, preferring to focus on the question of what meanings attach to particular objects, gestures, images, or utterances within the context of one specific ritual and one specific culture. Seen from this perspective, each of these ceremonies emerges as something that is intellectually profound, emotionally moving, and aesthetically beautiful, fully worthy of our attention and respect. I can only hope that I have begun to do justice to them.

Once analysis of data in their specificity is complete, however, comparison may be instructive. Beyond individual examples, these five rituals stand together as members of a broader set. All have the same goal—the transformation of an immature female into an adult—and consequently they share certain themes and together raise certain issues. Most important of these are the questions of what a woman is, what her traditional place is in society, and how ritual creates in individual women the willingness and ability to occupy that place. Such questions are profoundly disturbing in many respects, but ultimately must be addressed. In this regard, a study of women's rituals, however much it may focus on ritual, still inevitably says something about women.

I stated earlier that my chief goal was to raise the question of what women's rituals can tell us about ritual: its functions, forms, constituent parts; its mode of operation, logic, and scope; perhaps most of all, its meanings and strategies. A definition of ritual thus properly lies at the end of this inquiry, rather than at the beginning, but one inevitably works with provisional definitions at every step of the way. The best one can hope for is to make these provisional definitions explicit, maintaining the courage to revise them as required. For the moment, I view ritual as a coherent set of symbolic actions that has a real, transformative effect on individuals and social groups.[32] I am struck by such statements as that of John Gillin regarding a Pokomam woman for whom a healing ceremony had just been performed: "She seemed to have developed a new personality";[33] or that of Meyer Fortes regarding a Tallensi man who had been installed to tribal office: "Almost overnight, an ineffectual old man was turned into a dignified, self-confident, and authoritative, if somewhat garrulous, leader."[34]

Healing rituals and rituals of installation, like most rites of passage (including men's initiation), do what they claim to do: they transform people, replacing old roles, statuses, and identities with new ones, and in this regard women's initiation is much the same. But in women's initiation, a much more sweeping claim is also made, a claim characteristic of rites of renewal such as New Year's rites—to wit, that the cosmos itself is transformed along with the initiand. This audacious claim stands at the heart of the examples that follow, and will figure prominently in our final assessment of what women's initiation—and, beyond that, ritual in general—is and does.

Chapter

2

Tālikettukalyānam: The Marriage of Opposites

In North Kerala, a province located at the southern tip of the west coast of India, a rite is performed for young girls of the Tiyyar caste prior to their first menstrual period. The indigenous term for this ritual is *Tālikettukalyānam,* "the *tāli*-tying marriage," and the name is taken from the high point of the ceremony, the moment when a golden ornament (the *tāli*), which is the standard badge of marriage in South India, is tied around the girl's neck.[1] This simple action is sufficient to alter her life permanently, and as a result of it the girl becomes a woman, assumes new duties, is given a new honorific title (*amma,* "mature or married woman") and is considered eligible for marriage.[2] The ceremony is a gentle one in which friends and relatives show support and affection for the initiand.

Actually, the tāli-tying rite seems to have been a victim of modernization, last having been performed in the 1930s. In order to study it, therefore, we are dependent upon travelers' reports, testimony before the Malabar Marriage Commission of the 1890s, the writings of a few pioneer ethnologists, and the memories of those informants to whom more recent anthropologists had access. Yet for all the difficulties inherent in studying a rite that has not been performed in many years, a fairly clear picture of what was done has been pieced together, chiefly as the result of the work of Kathleen Gough, and the Tālikettukalyānam as practiced by the Tiyyars, the Nayars, and related groups throughout South India and Sri Lanka has been a favorite for study.[3] At one time or another, it has been assessed from psychoanalytic, sociological, and structuralist perspectives, and there is every indication of analyses yet to come.[4]

Given the extreme matrilineal pattern of organization among the

7

Tiyyars' caste superiors, the Nayar, whom A. R. Radcliffe-Brown called "the most thoroughgoing example of perpetual matrilineal succession,"[5] more attention has been directed to their tāli-tying rites than to those of any other group, although the Sinhalese rituals have received considerable scrutiny as well.[6] These examples are particularly well-documented, and they also offer fascinating evidence for questions relating to social hierarchy, marriage institutions, exogamy, kinship arrangements, and other issues dear to the heart of most social anthropologists.

One aspect of the Nayar rite that has most interested investigators is the question of whether it can be called a marriage, a "mock" marriage, a "fictive" marriage, or a "ritual" marriage, for many details of the symbolism point in this direction.[7] The Tiyyar tāli-tying, however, has much less of this, and for this reason some have been led to dismiss it as "a mere initiation ceremony"[8] or as being "relatively vague and confused."[9] It is just this fact, however—the predominance of initiatory significance and symbolism over that of marriage—that renders the northern Tiyyar practices of greatest interest to us.[10]

One way in which the Tiyyar tāli-tying does resemble the corresponding Nayar rite is that both must be performed before a girl reaches puberty. If this was not done and a girl began to menstruate before her tāli-tying had been held, in theory at least she would have been excommunicated from caste at that moment and never again accepted within society.[11] Underlying this extreme measure is an attempt to ensure the purity of the initiand, but also the avoidance of any possibility that she might enter into an anomalous status by accident, becoming an adult by physiological means while remaining a child by the standard of ritual. Of these two standards the latter is more important, for it is ceremony and not physiology that bestows social and religious maturity. Gough observes that as a result of the tāli-tying among the Nayar, "a girl was now thought to be at least ritually endowed with sexual and procreative functions, and was thenceforward accorded the status of a woman."[12] This was true even though a girl might have been quite young at the time of her initiation; there was no minimum age at which it could take place. Rather, the only specification had to do with the upper limit: the tāli-tying had to be performed before menarche.

Yet why the insistence on this point? Certainly most other cultures have handled the question differently by using physiological maturity as a sign that a child is ready for initiation and other forms of maturity as well.[13] But in South India there was no wavering on the issue: the ritual had to be accomplished before puberty, for religion makes adulthood more than does body chemistry. It was not simply a matter of showing preference for the sacred over the profane definition of adult status, however, although that is one thing to be considered. In insisting that the rite be performed prior to pubescence, the Tiyyar and Nayar affirmed that they, their ceremonies, and traditions made a girl a woman. Menstruation might commence at any time, and to permit adulthood to be so defined is tantamount to surrendering important human concerns to the whim of fate. Similarly, to wait until menarche and then perform initiation is little better, for in that event people's lives are still subject to the vagaries of time and chance. Seen from this perspective, the only way in which one can seriously claim to have taken the matter out of the hands of destiny is by performing initiation before there can be any chance of puberty, which is what the Nayar and Tiyyar did.

For the Nayar, this led to certain definitional problems because their tāli-tying in many ways functioned as a marriage as well as an initiation, and issues were raised similar to those involved in child-marriage as historically practiced elsewhere in India.[14] The Tiyyar, for their part, while retaining aspects of the ritual that might have marital reference, drastically deemphasized them and thus minimized such contradictions.[15] For them, the tāli-tying was primarily a rite of initiation, and in order to understand this we must turn to the details of the ceremony itself.[16]

Among the northern Tiyyar, the ritual of women's initiation lasted four days and began when the girl to be initiated was led to the inner room of her matrilineal ancestral house. This is the room in which menstruating women usually stay,[17] and there she remained secluded for three days, just as during menstruation. During this time, she observed the same taboos on eating or seeing certain things that were observed by menstruating women, and it thus appears that she was treated as if her first menses had taken place, a menarche, however, that was arranged by conscious decision and effected by ritual means rather than by the happenstance of physiology.

On the fourth day, a sacred pavilion (pandal) was built to house the ceremonies that followed, and on this morning the girl left her seclusion and went from the house to bathe at a nearby pool. At this pool, her brother planted an arrow in the earth with its tip up, "to drive away evil spirits."[18] After she bathed, the girl cut a coconut in half, then returned to her room in a festal procession.

Once back in the seclusion room, the girl was dressed and ornamented by a woman of the caste of barbers and washers, a caste lower than that of the Tiyyar but whose members play an indispensable role in purification practices by providing clean clothing, which in connection with a bath removes the pollution of birth, death, and menstruation.[19] They are the purifiers par excellence, and members of this caste appear throughout the tāli-tying rite, a chief goal of which is the establishment of purity in the initiand. Members of this caste repeatedly cleanse or provide clothing for the initiand, who will thus enter her new status free of pollution.[20] Rice was thrown over the girl as she dressed, and during this her maternal aunt (mother's brother's wife) placed a plank made from a latex-exuding tree commonly called the milk-tree (*Alstonia scholaris*) on a mat over husked and unhusked rice inside the pandal. This plank was to be the girl's seat during the ceremonies that followed.

Once dressed, the girl was led into the pandal and seated upon the milk-wood plank, where she made offerings of rice to the fire, the four cardinal directions, earth, and sky. A mud pot was brought out, and a number of small objects—coins, charcoal, foodstuffs, spices—were wrapped in leaves and placed into it. A leaf was placed over the top of the pot and fastened with string. The girl sprinkled the pot with rice, broke a hole through the leaf, and extracted one of the items (see Figure 1). This object was regarded as an omen of her destiny, and in particular was supposed to augur the number of children she would

Figure 1. Divination within the Tālikettukalyānam. The illustration shows the clay pot from which the initiand extracted one of several small objects. The object was then used to foretell her future.

bear. The girl was presented with gifts of new clothes, which she had
to share with the barber, who then anointed her hands with coconut
water.

When these preliminaries had been completed the tāli, hung on a
white silk thread, was tied around the girl's neck, and care was taken
so that this was done at an hour chosen as auspicious by the local as-
trologer. The tāli itself (Figure 2) is a small golden ornament shaped
like a leaf of the pipal tree (*Ficus religiosa*), the most sacred tree to both
Hindus and Buddhists. Among the Nayar and Tiyyar this tree is
worshipped as an embodiment of the god Vishnu, and it is said to
symbolize male creative power.[21] Usually it was the mother's
brother's wife who had the honor of tying on the tāli, although the
father's brother's wife, father's sister, or even the barber woman
might substitute. On the strength of the fact that the various female
relatives would be prospective mothers-in-law to the initiand, Gough
argued that the tying of the tāli by one of them was a symbolic marriage, in that the marriage emblem was tied by a member of the kinship group into which the girl would marry.[22] But such an interpretation cannot explain the barber woman's being allowed to tie the
tāli, for she comes from a lower caste into which the girl is forbidden
to marrry.[23] Really, all that can be said to explain the various people

Figure 2. The tāli, emblem of marriage throughout South India, as it
is worn by Tiyyar women. Based on a photograph in Thurston, *Ethnographic Notes in Southern India,* plate 36.

who may tie the tāli among the northern Tiyyar is that they are all women, but that alone is significant, for among all other groups reported it is a male who performs this highly significant gesture.[24]

After the tāli was tied, only a few more steps were needed to complete the ceremony. The barber woman poured water on the girl's hands as a final purification. Then the girl was asked to look at a lit cotton wick that was stuck to a coconut and compare this to the sun. When she had done so, she was taken outside in a procession led by this lamp and ushered to a coconut tree whose roots she watered. With this the ritual was complete and she was led back to the inner room of the ancestral house.

There are any number of details here that are of great interest. Several actions—such as seclusion of the initiand, public display of her in a festal procession, and repeated purifications—are found in many rites of women's initiation around the world. Others—the deliberate imitation of rites for menstruation, the milk-wood seat, and the alternation between two forms of sacred space, the old ancestral house and the newly constructed pandal—are equally fascinating but more limited in their dispersion. There are, however, three specific aspects of the ritual that I would like to dwell on: the divination by the clay pot, the tying of the tāli, and the water poured on the roots of the coconut tree.

The first of these is perhaps the most transparent in its symbolism, and the key to interpreting it is furnished by the identification of the object pulled from the pot with the number of children the girl would later bear. This identification leads to others, for if these objects are the children, then the pot that contains them can only be the woman's womb. Similarly, the leaf that covers the pot must be the woman's hymen, and her piercing the leaf in order to extract an object is her own symbolic self-defloration. Seen thus, the act is stunning in its implications. Here, even more than in the imitation of rites for menarche, the claim is made that this girl is not subject to fate, destiny, time, or whim; the specific actions that were to make a woman of her did not simply *happen*, but were arranged, controlled, organized, and performed within a ritual context. Moreover, with this gesture the girl affirmed that no male was necessary for her introduction to matters sexual. She herself was in control of her body, her sexuality, and her reproductive capability, and by breaking the leaf over the pot she announced this to all those assembled.

Later, when her menstruation actually did begin, a similar rite was performed for her by others, in which a fresh spathe of coconut and of areca palm were split open and the blossoms placed in a pot. If there were many blossoms, it augured well for her fertility.[25] Here—and, of course, when the act was physically performed—the "defloration" was not under her control. Yet these are of lesser importance, being the second or third time around. What matters is that the first, the *real* defloration was performed by the girl on herself without assistance or interference by others.

If this interpretation is correct, by the time the moment of the tāli-tying was reached, the initiand had symbolically menstruated and been introduced to sexuality, and was ready for "marriage," even though she might have been only eight or nine years old. Although the symbolism of marriage was much less pronounced among the northern Tiyyar than among other South Indian groups, we still cannot ignore the fact that the ceremony involves considerable nuptial imagery, the tāli being the emblem of marriage and the milk-wood plank being called the marriage-seat, for example.[26] This notwithstanding, the Tiyyar Tālikettukalyāṇam has much less nuptial symbolism than that of the Nayar (as has been emphatically pointed out by Yalman and Dumont), involving no ritual bridegroom, no intercourse, and no ritual divorce, unlike the Nayar rite. There is thus much less call to speak of the northern Tiyyar Tālikettukalyāṇam as a marriage than there is for the corresponding ceremony among any other group.[27] On the basis of this evidence, I am inclined to think of the northern Tiyyar rite as both being and not being a marriage, or perhaps—the most interesting possibility—being a marriage, but not in the same sense as the others.

In order to appreciate this, we should consider just what a marriage is. While detailed definitions have been proposed to cover all manner of variation in practice, a very general definition would point to marriage as a semipermanent union of a man or men with a woman or women, although even this loose fomulation fails to cover cases such as homosexual marriage or the marriage of a nun to Christ, to name two examples. One might even ask whether such a definition ought to be formulated in terms of persons at all. Certainly one can speak of marriages within the animal kingdom, and even within the realm of inanimate entities as well, such as the marriage of heaven and earth (Hesiod, et al.) or the marriage of flesh and air (Wallace Stevens). In these latter instances, what seems to be described is not a social arrangement of individual persons but rather a union of two opposite forces or entities that might—but need not necessarily—be described as male and female. This is to say that marriage, when understood at the broadest possible level, is not a familial or sexual arrangement, but is something metaphysical, being truly a *coincidentia oppositorum,* a fusion of opposites to create out of separateness a grander totality. It is this type of marriage, I would argue, that was celebrated for the north Tiyyar woman at her Tālikettukalyāṇam.[28]

In order to appreciate this, we must note that throughout the ceremony the initiand was repeatedly brought into association with symbols that were decidedly male. She was sprinkled with rice several times, symbolic of semen; she was presented with the phallic upright arrow planted in the earth by her brother;[29] and according to some sources she was given an arrow during her seclusion, an arrow said to be that of Kāma, god of desire.[30] This last practice corresponds to the Sinhalese practice described by Leach of giving the girl a rice pestle to keep with her in seclusion. Leach, however, denies that these items have any sexual reference, and argues that the pestle is simply an incomplete object, lacking the mortar that normally goes with it. The implication is that the girl at this stage of her initiation, like the pestle, is still incomplete.[31]

Leach's observation that both pestle and girl are incomplete is an astute one, but by refusing to recognize the phallic symbolism of the pestle (and the arrow among the Tiyyar) he overlooks the fact that their incompleteness is not parallel but complementary. The girl, being only female at this point, lacks the male; the pestle, being only male, lacks the female. When they are brought together a union of opposites takes place: a marriage. That this is specifically intended is indicated by the fact that in their ceremonies at menarche, an occasion that emphasizes only the female aspects of a woman, the Nayar isolate the girl with a bell-metal mirror, a common uterine symbol, instead of the phallic arrow appropriate for a ceremony that emphasizes the union of female and male.[32]

The prime example of this symbolic union of male and female, however, is the tying of the tāli itself, emblematic of the pipal tree, Vishnu, and male creative power. Quite often the pipal is associated as male to female with the margosa tree (*Melia azadirachta*), and the two are planted together in "marriage," so that the vines of the pipal can twine around the limbs of its mate.[33] The culminating act in women's initiation among the northern Tiyyar was thus the placing of a strongly marked masculine symbol around the neck of a young girl, and this act was called "the tāli-tying marriage" (Tālikettu-kalyānam).

This is a marriage in the sense that it is a union of opposites: the female who stands on the brink of maturity, and the male tāli. Such a marriage constitutes an initiatory act because of the understanding that the sexes—or opposites of any sort for that matter—never fully exist in separation from one another. Where opposites seem to exist independently, there is only an imperfect, inchoate state, and true perfection requires totality. Female alone or male alone is not the ideal, for it is only a part of the whole, and being merely a part it is not perfected, it is not mature.

The mature state, then, is that in which both male and female are present in union. Initiation as the rite in which an immature individual is perfected and brought to adulthood involves, among the northern Tiyyar, the fusing of male and female. A girl becomes a woman by becoming whole, by being defined in opposition to and in union with male elements, and this is done by tying the tāli on her. Thereafter, she will never take it off unless she is widowed, becoming once again an incomplete and imperfect person.[34]

We have yet to examine the actions that took place at the coconut tree at the end of the ceremony. Having been ritually brought to menarche, deflowered, and married, the initiand had to go outside and pour water on the roots of a coconut tree before her initiation was complete. What sense is to be found in this simple gesture?

In order to answer this question, it is helpful to consider the water-pouring together with the parts of the ritual inside the pandal which immediately preceded it. Here, unfortunately, the reporting of Gough—normally so excellent—breaks down, for she was really interested in other things. Fortunately, however, we do have the account of Thurston and Rangachari, which is more complete on this point. According to them, after the tāli had been tied and the girl's hands washed, "a cotton wick, steeped in oil, is then twisted round a piece of bamboo, and stuck on a young cocoanut. The girl is asked if she sees the sun, looks at the lighted wick, and says that she does" (see Figure 3).[35] This makes little sense except as preparation for what was to come, for this was the establishment of a symbolic equation that acquired added significance in the next steps of the rite: the coconut

Figure 3. The solar coconut.

was identified with the sun by virtue of its spherical shape and the flame placed on top of it. Were this not sufficient, the identification was suggested to the initiand with a leading question, and she then affirmed it for all the audience by her response.

It was with this homology in mind, then, that the girl and her attendants left the pandal for a tree outside. The tree, of course, could not be just any tree but had to be a coconut tree, and it was here that the equation of coconut and sun was pursued to greatest advantage. For if the coconuts hanging from the tree's branches were also seen as the sun, then the tree itself could only be the cosmic tree—a common image in India and in the general history of religions—which stands at the center of the earth, supports the heavens, connects all the realms of the universe, and provides food for all living creatures.[36] On a more pedestrian level, one should recall that the traditional occupation of the Tiyyar caste is toddy-tapping, that is, the procurement of sap from a related species of palm tree, which was then sold to dealers for use in the preparation of liquors and candy.[37] In a very real sense, then, Tiyyar livelihood and well-being depended on the palm tree in its terrestrial and its cosmic sense. The initiand stood at the very foot of this all-important tree and poured water on its roots, giving it life and strength, thus helping to secure the welfare of her people and support the entire cosmos, a task entrusted only to the most prestigious figures by other cultures—the king in Mesopotamia, and the Norns or Fates in ancient Scandinavia.[38]

Among the Tiyyar, however, this awesome responsibility was delegated to each girl as she came of age. She was able to assume this responsibility by virtue of her initiation, being no longer a girl, but a woman. Having been incomplete and underage, she was made whole, perfect, and pure. She was made mature in the course of the ritual, and became ready to take on responsibility for nothing less than the maintenance of the entire universe, something she began by pouring water on the roots of a coconut tree.

A Tiyyar woman in north Kerala had many responsibilities. She was expected to bear children who would continue the matrilineal line and to raise them until they were old enough to return to their ancestral home. She was expected to feed her family, and all cooking was done by women only. Also, unlike the Nayar woman, she was expected to do a great deal of agricultural work, and most of the harvesting was in her hands.[39] In all these ways she supported life and sustained the creation, and the tāli tied round her neck was the sign that she was prepared for these responsibilities.

Chapter

3

Kinaaldá: Becoming the Goddess

Among the Navajo a young girl's first menstruation is cause for general rejoicing, because it indicates that she is ready to bring forth new life.[1] As Gladys Reichard put it, menarche "is regarded as the fulfillment of a promise, the attainment of reproductive power."[2] Physiological maturity alone, however, is not sufficient for the fulfillment of this promise. The girl must also be ritually transformed, made over, before she takes her place as a woman. Puberty is a precondition for the performance of the initiation rite called *Kinaaldá* ("first menstruation," or perhaps "house sitting," with reference to the intiand's stay within her family hogan),[3] but it is this rite—performed for each girl at her first two periods—that is believed to bestow the power of bearing children. Frank Mitchell, one of the most knowledgeable Navajo informants, observed that "the ceremony was started so women would be able to have children and the human race would be able to multiply,"[4] or, as a more detached observer rather blandly put it, "Its obvious intent is to prepare the girl for future motherhood."[5]

The Navajo religious system is extremely rich in ceremonial, and there have been numerous attempts to classify its various divisions. The Navajo themselves differentiate two major "song ceremonial complexes" from the rest of their various chants, and set these in marked opposition to each other. The first is known as "Enemyway," and it is used in rituals of exorcism, warfare, and healing, among others, being designed primarily for the overcoming of adversity in one form or another. The second group, known as "Blessingway," is used in rites whose emphasis is on the creation or preservation of a state of harmony, peace, and well-being: those for the birth of a child, the erection of a hogan, a wedding, and so forth.[6]

17

Each of these song cycles recounts an elaborate mythology believed to be particularly relevant to the rituals governed by that cycle. Enemyway tells of the twin culture heroes and how they vanquished all manner of threatening monsters, while Blessingway deals with the birth of a goddess, Changing Woman (also known as White Shell Woman or Turquoise Woman in certain contexts),[7] detailing how she was born, grew to maturity, and became the mother of the twins whose exploits are related in Enemyway. Blessingway thus seems to have a certain logical priority over Enemyway, and the Navajo regard the former as the most important of their chants, on which Enemyway and all others ultimately depend. In the words of Long Mustache, "It is the spinal column of songs."[8]

Of all the rites based upon the Blessingway cycle, none is more important than the Kinaaldá, regarded by some as the most important of all Navajo ceremonies.[9] As a part of the Blessingway complex, Kinaaldá is directed toward the obtaining of good fortune, happiness, and perfection; all mention of anything related to illness, conflict, or unpleasantness is strictly forbidden.[10] In the course of the ritual, which lasts four nights and five days, only Blessing Songs are sung, "which are the holiest,"[11] and all the ritual events are patterned after those of the first and second Kinaaldá, which, according to Blessingway, were performed for Changing Woman.

Most of the ceremony takes place inside the initiand's family hogan. On one level, this hogan is simply the regular family dwelling, and as such familiar and comfortable for the kinaaldá girl. But in the course of the ritual it takes on new significance as a result of the songs that are chanted. It is extremely difficult for us to comprehend the importance of these, given the gulf that separates our world-view from that of the Navajo, and a full treatment of the importance of song in Navajo ideology could fill volumes.[12] Briefly, however, the Navajo analysis might be summarized as follows. Knowledge is regarded as the fundamental support of the universe, and as such it contains inestimable creative power. As a rule, this knowledge finds its expression in thought, which in turn is expressed in speech, the highest form of which is song. To put it in the terms the Navajo use, speech is the "outer form" of thought, and thought the "inner form" of speech, while thought and knowledge also stand in the relation of outer form : inner form to one another. It thus follows that the speech of one who has full knowledge and has perfected his or her thought is rich in creative power and can effectively remake the world. The chief singer at any ritual is expected to be such a person, and his or her songs—which are largely traditional and drawn from mythic lore—re-create the world of the present in the image of the world and time of myths.

An "all-night sing" fills the final night of the Kinaaldá. The first songs sung are called Hogan Songs, which were composed for the Kinaaldá of Changing Woman, according to Blessingway. By means of these songs, the mythic characters First Man and First Woman sang the primordial hogan into existence.[13] Hogan Songs of the present repeat this event, and the singer's words simultaneously secure the continued existence of the family hogan, make it holy, and identify it with the first hogan, which was located at Emergence Rim, the place where the Holy People first issued from a series of underworlds onto the earth's surface. In one Hogan Song, Frank Mitchell chants:

> heye nene yana (invocation)
> I fully understand it, I fully understand it,
> I fully understand it, I fully understand it.
>
> Now with my doorway, now with my door curtain,
>   the house has come into being it is said.
>   I fully understand it, I fully understand it,
>   I fully understand it, I fully understand it.[14]

Having started at the doorway, he goes on to construct the frame and crossbeams through song, fills the hogan with necessities (fire, food, dishes, broom, bedding, and so forth), and adds the prototypes of luxury (soft fabrics and jewels). Finally he concludes:

> Now long life, now everlasting beauty,
>   were brought into the interior, it is said.
>   I fully understand it, I fully understand it,
>   I fully understand it.
>
>   I fully understand it, I fully understand it,
>   I fully understand it, I fully understand it, it is said.[15]

The hogan is thus transformed into the first hogan by the knowledge and speech of the singer. Its space becomes sacred space, and all who enter it once again stand at Emergence Rim. Through this experience, they themselves are also transformed and take on something other than their normal workaday existence—becoming nothing less than the gods and Holy People who dwelt at Emergence Rim. This is most important for the initiand. Once inside the hogan, she has her hair combed so that it hangs down her back fixed with an archaic form of thong, and she is dressed in ceremonial finery—a special sash and jewelry of turquoise and white shell being particularly prominent—in order to make her over in the image of Changing Woman.[16] This dressing is accompanied by, or perhaps better yet, accomplished by songs, as for instance the following, in which the initiand is identified as the child of Changing Woman and is dressed and ornamented like Changing Woman herself:

Now the child of Changing Woman,
   now she has dressed her up,
In the center of the Turquoise house,
   now she has dressed her up . . .
Turquoise Girl, now she has dressed her up,
Her turquoise shoes, now she has dressed her up,
Her turquoise leggings now she has dressed her up,
Her turquoise clothes, now she has dressed her up . . .
She is decorated with jewels, now she has dressed her up,
She is decorated with soft fabrics, now she has dressed her up,

Behind her it is blessed; now she has dressed her up,
Before her, it is blessed; now she has dressed her up,
Now the girl of long life and everlasting beauty,
   now she has dressed her up.[17]

Once she has been dressed, the girl is given a rigorous massage by several older women of known good character. This action is repeated at various times throughout the Kinaaldá and is referred to as "molding" the initiand, a practice based upon the belief that at the time of initiation a girl's body becomes soft again, as it was at birth, and she is thus susceptible to being literally re-formed by the efforts of those around her.[18] Keith reports one extremely old woman she knew who attributed a newly painful leg to a fall she suffered during her Kinaaldá sixty years earlier.[19]

After all this preparation, the kinaaldá girl is ready to undertake certain actions required of her. Standing at her ceremonial position in the western end of the hogan, facing east, she greets a series of visitors, each of whom she lifts upward, thus imparting some of the power of growth with which she abounds at this moment in her life.[20] This done, she leaves the hogan to run a race with other young people along a prescribed pattern: eastward from the hogan toward the sun, a sunwise turn (clockwise or deasil), and a return westward to the hogan, with the initiand always in the lead. The race is, in effect, her pursuit of the sun.

Later in the day the kinaaldá girl runs again, and for the next three days she runs three times each day. On these days she has little to do except run and grind corn for the enormous cake (*alkaan*) that will be consumed on the morning of the fifth day. Running and grinding are both strenuous, and the girl is expected to work hard at them. Part of the reason for this is the explicit desire to make her industrious in later life, and the inclusion of such requirements moved Harold Driver to classify the Kinaaldá as belonging to the "work complex" type of female initiation in North America.[21] But underlying this apparently mundane motive is an essentially religious perception: that of initiation as a time of rebirth during which the individual is created anew. Just as she may be physically "molded," so also may her character be re-formed, and it is toward this end that her labor is directed.

All of these actions are directly patterned on those of Changing Woman at her Kinaaldá, as related in Blessingway. She, too, had her hair combed, was dressed, was "molded," ran, and ground corn. Wyman describes the initiation of the goddess as a "prototype ceremonial,"[22] and, according to Blessingway traditions, upon the completion of this first Kinaaldá the Holy People in attendance announced, "This ceremony which has been performed for Changing Woman will be [for] people in that shape, all of us [future Navajos] will be in this shape,"[23] which is to say that forever afterward the rite would be performed as it had been established in the beginning.

On the fourth day of the ceremony, work begins on a part of the ritual that is given only slight mention in the myths, yet which is of the greatest importance. Some of the men present dig a large circular pit, as much as six feet in diameter, to the east of the hogan, and a fire is kept going inside it all day. Toward evening the fire is allowed to die down, and the ashes are raked out. The kinaaldá girl places a cross made from four husks of corn at the center of the pit, with points oriented to the cardinal directions. From this cross, the women lay a network of husks over the bottom of the pit with all of the tips pointing sunwise, and an enormous quantity of sweet cornmeal batter is poured in until the pit is filled. This batter is made from the corn that the kinaaldá girl has been grinding and from corn ground by other women. Water, sugar, and raisins are added, and also a bit of corn pollen, "the emblem of peace, of happiness, of prosperity."[24] The initiand herself mixes this batter, but others carry it to the pit and pour it in, being careful to pour it in a sunwise circular direction. Once the batter is all in the pit, the initiand blesses it with ceremonial corn meal, scattered in a sunwise circle.[25] The batter is covered with husks, in the center of which the initiand places another corn-husk cross oriented to the cardinal points. Moist earth is shoveled in to cover the batter, a fire is built up on top and kept going all night long to bake the batter fully.

By the time the fire has been rebuilt it is the evening of the fourth day, when the Kinaaldá moves toward its climax. Beginning around eleven o'clock all those involved in the ceremony assemble at the family's hogan, where they spend the entire night singing and listening to the sacred Blessingway songs. Seating in the hogan is rigidly ordered (Figure 4). In the west are the kinaaldá girl and the chief singer, who leads the evening's action. In front of them is a blanket on which are

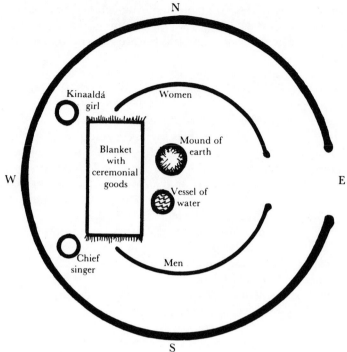

N

W   E

S

Figure 4. Plan of the hogan as arranged for the all-night sing. Adapted from Frisbie, *Kinaaldá,* p. 49.

items to be blessed. In the hogan's center are a mound of earth and a pail of water, representing those fundamental elements. To the north sit all the women, to the south the men. The east is left open, and the doorway to the hogan is located there; at dawn the first rays of the sun will enter through this door, just as Sun came to Changing Woman through her hogan's eastern door at the beginning of time.

Once all the participants have arrived the hogan is blessed with corn pollen, which is then passed in a sunwise circle so that all in attendance may bless themselves. Singing begins with the Hogan Songs, of which there are two sorts: Chief Hogan Songs, used in a girl's first Kinaaldá, and Talking God Hogan Songs, used in her second. Of the two, the Talking God Hogan Songs are perhaps the more interesting. Frisbie observes:

> The Talking God Songs progress as follows: the house where the Blessing Way Ceremony is taking place first becomes a ceremonial hogan, a sacred place. This house is next identified with that of a particular deity . . . By Song No. 13, the house has become that of Changing Woman (and White Shell Woman), and this deity is

moving toward it. In Song No. 25, she reaches the house, which is now thoroughly beautified and sanctified through decorations, various kinds of prayer offerings, and the presence of many deities. At this point, the person referred to in the song text is no longer "she"; instead, it is "I"—an "I" which is now completely identified with the chief Kinaaldá deity.[26]

The text of the dramatic Talking God Hogan Song 25 reads in part as follows:

> *haiye naiye yana* [invocation]
> With my sacred power, I am traveling,
> With my sacred power, I am traveling,
> With my sacred power, I am traveling.
> At the back of my house, white shell prayer offerings are placed;
>   they are beautifully decorated;
> With my sacred power, I am traveling,
> At the center of my house, turquoise prayer offerings are placed;
>   they are beautifully decorated;
> With my sacred power, I am traveling . . .
> All about my house is Talking God; He is beautifully clad;
>   With my sacred power, I am traveling,
> All about my house is Hogan God; She is beautifully clad;
>   With my sacred power, I am traveling . . .
>
> With beauty before me, I am traveling,
>   With my sacred power, I am traveling,
> With beauty behind me, I am traveling,
>   With my sacred power, I am traveling,
> With beauty below me, I am traveling,
>   With my sacred power, I am traveling,
> With beauty above me, I am traveling,
>   With my sacred power, I am traveling,
> Now with long life, now with everlasting beauty, I live.
>   I am traveling,
> With my sacred power, I am traveling.[27]

Other songs follow: the "free singing," in which anyone may offer a song, and the Twelve Word Songs which wipe out any possible errors in the preceding steps of the rite. When these songs are concluded the sun is rising, and the chief singer introduces the Dawn Songs or Washing Songs. The latter name is due to the fact that while they are sung the hair and the jewelry of the kinaaldá girl are washed—that is, the features by which she has been physically identified with Changing Woman are cleansed and renewed. A final race is run, accompanied by Racing Songs which chart the initiand's progress on her course. Another Twelve Word Song brings the all-night sing to a close.[28]

Throughout the singing, the chief goal is the identification of the initiand with Changing Woman, as most dramatically announced in the following Twelve Word Song:

> I am here; I am White Shell Woman, I am here.
> Now on the top of Gobernador Knob, I am here.
> In the center of my white shell hogan I am here.
> Right on the white shell spread I am here.
> Right on the fabric spread I am here.
> Right at the end of the rainbow I am here.[29]

When the singing has concluded, the participants bless themselves again with corn pollen and leave the hogan for the pit in which the cake has been baking all night. Once unearthed, the cake is cut into pieces, the first being taken from the eastern edge, with the knife always traveling in a sunwise direction. As the pieces are lifted out, the kinaaldá girl gives one to everyone, although she herself may not taste of it, despite the fact that throughout the ceremony she is forbidden to eat everything except foods made from corn.[30]

Most Navajo regard the ceremony as complete when the alkaan has been served and eaten, but there are a few steps that follow.[31] The initiand's hair is combed again, to the accompaniment of Combing Songs, and her body is painted with white clay, an upward motion always being used. She then paints the cheeks of all those who desire it, again using an upward stroke to extend some of her superabundant powers of growth to others.[32] Painting Songs are sung, and afterward her body is given a last molding. All these actions were also a part of the Kinaaldá of Changing Woman, as related in Blessingway.

Some time later, when all have departed, either one small piece from the center of the cake or four pinches from the pieces adjacent to the center are buried in a hole dug at the center of the pit. With regard to this gesture Frank Mitchell observed, "The cake belongs to the earth; these pieces are buried as a sacrifice to the earth and as an offering . . . That is done in order to be thankful for the harvest and for raising corn on the earth."[33]

Virtually all the actions performed in the Kinaaldá actively repeat the events of Changing Woman's Kinaaldá. That ceremony was the first such rite ever performed, and thus established the pattern for all to follow.[34] Performance of the rite in the present, however, is more than just faithful imitation of a traditional model. Rather, the happenings of the first time are re-created by means of the ritual songs and actions: the family hogan becomes the first hogan, the guests at the all-night sing become the Holy People, and the kinaaldá girl becomes Changing Woman.

The importance of this identification has been noted by many authorities,[35] and Driver maintained that it is one of the central features of women's initiation among the Athabascan tribes of the American Southwest, a group that includes the Navajo. Driver's interpretation, however, seems rather pale and pedestrian: "During the entire ceremony she [the initiand] impersonates a culture heroine in the hope that she will become as virtuous and successful."[36] No doubt virtue and success are desired and are one goal of the rite, but the initiand gains a good deal more than these mundane personal benefits by ritually becoming—not just "impersonating"—Changing Woman.

Changing Woman herself is an extremely complex figure. Probably the most important of all Navajo deities, she has also been called the most fascinating of them by Gladys Reichard: "No matter how much we know about her the total is a great question mark. She is the mystery of reproduction, of life springing from nothing, of the last hope of the world, a riddle perpetually solved and perennially springing up anew."[37] Her name, which might be translated more literally as "the woman who is transformed time and again," is given in recognition of a peculiarity of her life cycle: she grows old and becomes young again with the flow of the seasons.[38] One might thus interpret her as an allegory of the seasons, but she is more, being also related to the earth and vegetation.

> Slim Curly said, "Thereby the earth, when vegetation appears in the spring, becomes as a young woman clothed in a new dress, whereas harvest in the fall lets her appear as a declining old woman. White Shell Woman is, in reality, the earth which changes in summer and becomes young again, then relaxes or dies off in winter." He called the earth, "Changing Woman Happiness" for summer and "Changing Woman Long Life" in winter.[39]

Here, vegetation is regarded as the dress of Changing Woman. Elsewhere, the connection is portrayed as even closer, the cycle of the crops being seen as "a function of Changing Woman's annual rejuvenation,"[40] or as a gift from the goddess to humanity: "She called the people of the clans her children and promised them corn of all colors and plant seed; so now when corn doesn't grow and ripen, women, too, will not give birth, for all seeds and corn originate with White Shell Woman."[41] This last text hints at the connection of human and vegetative fertility, both of which originate in and are controlled by Changing Woman. But a still stronger point could be made: all fertility is hers, for as First Woman said of Changing Woman, "Whatever is on the earth's surface, and the means of making life possible, have all been given into her charge."[42]

A summary description such as this, however, only begins to give an idea of Changing Woman's complexity. In order to better appreciate it, it is helpful to consider her mythology, pieces of which are related in both Enemyway and Blessingway. In Enemyway it is told that Changing Woman appeared at a crucial moment in world history, being born shortly after the Holy People emerged to the earth's surface from the last underworld below. At that time the Holy People were being exterminated by various monsters that had come into being "through the fault of the women."[43] It seems that certain women had conceived monsters while masturbating: a woman who masturbated with an elk's horn produced a horned monster, one who used a feather gave birth to a monstrous eagle, and so forth. These monsters grew rapidly and preyed mercilessly upon the Holy People, threatening them with extinction.[44] It was to rectify this situation that Changing Woman was born so that she might become the mother of the hero twins, who would ultimately exterminate the monsters. This is stated explicitly in Enemyway and certain versions of Blessingway, although properly no mention of the monsters should appear in the latter.[45] Some informants thus offer a more general motivation for Changing Woman's birth, such as Frank Mitchell's oblique statement that "some were not keeping things holy as it should be."[46]

Although this last statement may appear to be mere euphemism, something more subtle is at work: the observation and preservation of the separate ritual categories of Enemyway and Blessingway. Although more veiled than the other, Frank Mitchell's statement makes the same point in terms acceptable within Blessingway: Changing Woman was born to bring propriety, safety, and civilization into existence. Seen thus, she represents the triumph of cosmos over chaos, humanity over monsters, and productive, mature sexuality over the dangers of adolescent masturbation. Here, as in numerous other mythologies (for example, Hesiod's *Theogony*), birth by parthenogenesis is understood to be extremely dangerous, producing one-sided monsters who lack the balance of those creatures born out of the union of the sexes.

For her part, Changing Woman was conceived and born in miraculous fashion. River Junction Curly begins the story as follows:

Gobernador Knob [one of the sacred mountains located around Emergence Rim] was covered by dark clouds, they say. Its peak was enveloped with dark clouds all over. A black fog was also with this. It [the peak] could not be seen as it sits, they say. There were also rainbows floating around and some red sun halos appeared, they say. Sunbeams also extended, they say. This was discovered at dawn, they say. It was merely like that and it was watched for four days, they say. This was being watched from these holy places for four days, they say. People wondered why this was like that. "There must be some explanation," they said when it was discussed.[47]

This conjunction of cloud and mountaintop is clearly meant as a sexual union, complete with attendant fireworks. Most informants have interpreted it as the joining of heaven and earth, and some have pushed the analysis further, seeing cloud and mountain peak as the "outer forms," or external representations of earth and sky, the "inner forms" or underlying essence of earth and sky being the true parents of Changing Woman.[48] In any event, Changing Woman was born at the end of the four days and was found on top of the mountain by First Man, who went to investigate the strange happenings.

Earth and sky are presented as opposite entities in Navajo myth and iconography. Earth is female; sky, male; earth, below; heaven, above; earth faces eastward, having dawn for her headplume; sky faces west, with twilight for his.[49] Sandpaintings of the pair show Mother Earth containing sacred plants, particularly corn, in her body, while Father Sky's body is filled with the sun, moon, and stars. Yet for all their differences, they appear quite similar and are joined close together by a pollen path (Figure 5). Their mating, then, is a *hieros gamos,* a sacred marriage in which complementary opposites are united, and Changing Woman is the product of this union.

Taken to the home of First Man and First Woman, Changing Woman grew to maturity in a remarkably short time (as little as four days in some versions)[50] and the first Kinaaldá was held for her, with all the deities in attendance, at Emergence Rim—the center of the earth and also its vagina, from which the Holy People first issued forth. At the end of the ceremony the gods proclaimed that every future kinaaldá must be performed just as was that of Changing Woman. In one version of Blessingway, however, Changing Woman herself established her kinaaldá as the model for all to follow, telling the first Navajo, "After this, all the girls born to you will have periods at certain times when they become women. When the time comes, you must set a day and must fix the girl up to be kinaaldá; you must have these songs sung and do whatever else needs to be done at that time. After this period a girl is a woman and will start having children."[51]

By virtue of her kinaaldá Changing Woman became ready to have children, but her fertility was not limited to this alone.[52] At the outset of her initiation it was said that "this one shall now be made holy [so that] in the future, life can be regulated by her,"[53] and she was told that if all were done correctly "there will be birth. Vegetation, as well

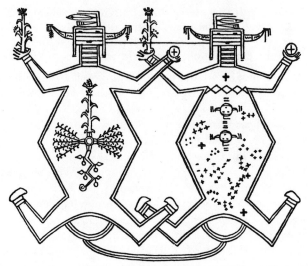

Figure 5. Sand painting of Mother Earth (left) and Father Sky (right). The two figures are virtually identical. Their fundamental unity is also stressed by the pollen path, symbol of prayer, that connects their mouths, and the lines that connect their genitals, signifying their sexual union. From Newcomb, Fishler, and Wheelwright, *A Study of Navajo Symbolism*, p. 19.

as all without exception who travel the surface of the earth, will give birth, that you will have gained."[54] All fertility thus depends upon that of Changing Woman, which was won through the Kinaaldá. As a replication of Changing Woman in the present, each kinaaldá girl bears the same responsibility and holds the same powers.

Changing Woman's initiation thus prepared her to support the birth of all things, and the drypaintings made in conjunction with Blessingway show her ritually attired with loose hair, ceremonial sash, and whiteshell jewelry, flanked by high corn as an emblem of her universal fertility (Figure 6). On the most immediate level, however, she was made ready to become the mother of the hero twins who would rid the world of monsters. They story of how she conceived them, however, is no less complex than that of her own conception.

Accounts vary somewhat, but all agree that the sun was the father of the firstborn of the twins, Monster Slayer. According to some a sunray entered the vagina of Changing Woman while she was working, and according to others Sun appeared to her as a handsome youth with whom she lay.[55] More detailed accounts state that the Sun spoke to her while she was running the third of her races, thus pro-

Figure 6. Sand painting of Changing Woman. The goddess, dressed in ceremonial garb—loose hair, belt, necklaces (one assumes the thong to be in her hair, but this would not be visible from a full front view)—stands under a blue and yellow sunray arc, flanked by tall corn. Such paintings are very rare, being made only for Blessingway ceremonials. Only four have ever been collected, and those were given to Maud Oakes with the greatest reluctance because "they are very holy." Usually two such paintings are made together in a cornfield, the first for a man and the second for a woman. Together they are expected to ensure good crops and rain. From Wyman, *Blessingway* (copyright 1970), p. 75. Adapted by permission of the University of Arizona Press.

viding a rationale for the initiand's running toward the sun three times each day.[56] Still others make Sun a youth who approached Changing Woman and told her to prepare a circle of boughs with an opening to the east and lie there with her head to the west, so that he might come to her—a detail that explains the seating arrangement at the all-night sing.[57]

Having lain with Sun—whom Reichard wrongly characterizes as "an idealized philanderer," due to his ability to appear to any woman at any time—Changing Woman became pregnant with Monster Slayer.[58] The paternity of the second twin, Born for Water, is somewhat ambiguous, however. One version of the myth tells that while bathing after her tryst with Sun, Changing Woman allowed a moon-beam to shine on her vagina, but most others state that during her bath she allowed water to drip into her genitals and conceived as a result of this.[59] In any event, nine days later she gave birth to the twins. Blessingway has little to tell of their exploits, being concerned with peaceful things only, but Enemyway picks up here to tell how they rid the world of monsters. The story of Changing Woman and how she became mother of the twins, however, is crucial to both chant cycles, and she is the one character who figures prominently in both, being in this regard yet again a fusion of opposites.

This ideology of Changing Woman as a being in whom contraries are merged undergirds the stories of the twins' conception, for both variants tell how a union of opposites took place within her body. In one, the union is between the two heavenly luminaries, sun and moon. In the other (which seems to be older, in view of Born for Water's name) two opposing elements are joined—the celestial, fiery sun and the terrestrial, moist water. Both elements are necessary for life, and Changing Woman provides the matrix in which they can merge and be productive.

In this image of *coincidentia oppositorum* Changing Woman plays something of a passive role, being little more than a catalytic agent who makes possible the union of other elements.[60] But the myth is often viewed from a different perspective, in which the role of water or moon tends to be minimized.[61] When this is the case, Changing Woman's character is brought into bolder relief, and she herself is perceived as the opposite force brought into union with the sun. To-gether they form a second-generation union of opposites after Earth and Sky, much as Kronos and Rheia form a second-generation union of opposites after Ouranos and Gaia in Greek mythology.

Changing Woman's chief concern is fertility of all kinds—the ebb and flow of birth, death, and rebirth—and in this respect she is simi-lar to the sun, who is also much concerned with the bestowing of new life and with the rhythms of plants and seasons.[62] But if the two are to be grouped together in this regard, there is another way in which they must be seen as opposite or complementary forces. The sun may be understood as the embodiment of downward motion, whose beams originate on high and descend toward the earth bearing warmth, en-ergy, and life. In contrast, Changing Woman is the embodiment of upward motion, growth from the earth up toward the sky. This power she imparts to vegetation and humanity alike, as seen in two mo-ments from the Kinaaldá ritual: the initiand's lifting of others to make them grow, and the painting of her face with an upward stroke, which is said to aid the growth of plants.[63] The initiand is able to communicate this force because within the context of the rite she *is* Changing Woman.

This identification of the initiand with the Changing Woman of myth is the most important general theme of the Kinaaldá. It is accomplished through songs, through the initiand's dress and coiffure (compare Figure 6 and Figure 7), and through the conscious repetition of the first Kinaaldá. As a result, all fertility comes to depend on

Figure 7. Kinaaldá girl running one of the ceremonial races. In this picture, the girl's ceremonial garb is evident: necklaces, jewelry, hair hanging loose, held only by a thong partially visible above her left shoulder. In all these particulars, she repeats the dress of Changing Woman. Based on a photograph in McCombe, Vogt, and Kluckhohn, *Navaho Means People,* p. 59.

the kinaaldá girl: her own, that of her people, of the crops, and "everything that exists on the surface of the earth." Civilization, too, depends on her, for her future children are implicitly identified with the hero twins.

All of this follows from consideration of the Blessingway myths, noting their close connections to the steps of the Kinaaldá. But there is one event in the ceremony that is given scant mention, if any, in Blessingway, but which is nevertheless of the utmost importance: the preparation of the sweet corn cake (alkaan).[64]

The symbolism of this cake is extremely elaborate. Given its shape, color, and relation to fire, it must be seen as a solar image, a conclusion reinforced by informants' statements that it is baked as an offering to the sun, out of respect for the sun, or—most significant of all— "so it will be like the sun."[65]

This solar cake is baked in a subterranean pit—that is, within the body of the earth (earth consistently being considered female and sun male in Navajo thought).[66] On one level, this is reminiscent of the way in which the cake is made through the cooperative labor of the sexes, the pit being dug by men and the batter prepared and poured by women. Beyond this, in view of the identification of the family hogan with the first hogan, it is perhaps not too daring to see the pit from which the cake is taken as identified with Emergence Rim, the womb of the earth.[67]

If the extraction of the cake thus recalls the emergence of the Holy People, it also suggests the growth of the plants, for the alkaan is made of corn, the most sacred of all plants, and representative of the whole realm of vegetation.[68] By itself, corn is suggestive of life; in the sweet corn cake, it represents a happy and blessed existence. One also must consider the corn-husk crosses, which provide a sacred orientation, pointing to the four quarters and themselves located at top and bottom along the central axis.

The cake is thus an extremely complex symbolic cluster. It contains sun and earth; male and female; the Holy People, first of all beings; corn, and by extension all vegetation; the cardinal points; zenith and nadir. These diverse elements are integrated in an image of perfect totality, and the festive distribution and consumption of the cake after the rigorous all-night sing serves to integrate all the participants into the social totality as well.[69]

There is, however, one participant who does not join in this totality, but stands apart from it. This is the kinaaldá girl, who is forbidden to taste the cake but who serves it to the others, almost as if it is her own product she is offering.[70] In a sense, this is the case, for through the Kinaaldá she has become Changing Woman, become the earth, become the power of fertility in all things, and become upward growth. If the cake has been produced in the womb of the earth and emerges from that womb, it has been born from the initiand's womb as well. And if the cake is to be understood as an image of perfect totality, life, and well-being, these qualities now have their origin in her, just as they have always had their origin in Changing Woman.

When the Kinaaldá has been completed, the initiand is considered ready to marry and to have children.[71] Like her Tiyyar counterpart, the Navajo woman occupies a place of great importance and respect in society. Descent is determined through the maternal line, and residence is regularly matrilocal.[72] Ownership of the land belongs to women, insofar as one can speak of "ownership" among the Navajo, and the planting of crops is women's work, although men may assist.[73] Clyde Kluckhohn and Dorothea Leighton argued that Navajo respect for women was one of the chief factors in the Navajo's resistance to Christianity: "The Bible speaks only of a male God and of a society where authority and responsibility centers chiefly in men. Navahos miss Changing Woman, perhaps the principal Navaho divinity, and the whole feeling for the position of women embodied alike in their own social organization and religious lore."[74]

The perception is an astute one, but a stronger point could have been made. Social and religious factors are not separate, but inextricably tied. Respect for Changing Woman and respect for women in general are one and the same, for each woman *is* Changing Woman, and becomes so through performance of the Kinaaldá rite.

4

Tiv
Scarification:
The Pattern
of Time

One of the chief difficulties in any study of ritual is simply knowing what constitutes a ritual and what does not: the distinction is not always self-evident. Some rituals are easily recognized by their solemnity, sacerdotal supervision, sumptuous regalia, and elaborate rules for behavior. Other rituals may lack all these features, and even such apparently pedestrian actions as repairing a drum or cutting one's fingernails may on occasion be invested with the most profound ritual significance.[1]

It may be argued, of course, that this difficulty is only the result of unfamiliarity with a given culture, and that if one has recourse to knowledgeable informants the situation can easily be rectified. Such a solution, however, overlooks what might be termed unconscious ritual: those traditional patterns of behavior that are like ritual in all other respects—using symbolic action, transforming the individuals involved, endowing mundane existence with some grander meaning, and reaffirming the abstract values of society at large—but that for one reason or another are not recognized as rituals by those who practice them. To take a few examples from our own culture, how many twentieth-century American informants would identify shaking hands or brushing one's teeth as rituals? Yet the ritual dimension of these and similar acts has been convincingly demonstrated.[2] Turning to the topic of women's initiations, how many Americans would consider graduation from high school or college, debuts, sweet sixteen parties, bridal and baby showers, weddings, or even first dates as ritual events? Informants' opinions notwithstanding, all of the above could well be discussed from this perspective.

The Tiyyar Tālikettukalyānam and the Navajo Kinaaldá present

no major difficulties of this nature. Both are consciously understood
as ritual occasions by all participants and could be recognized as such
by most outside observers. These rites are spectacular affairs, elaborate in their execution and steeped in sacrality at every turn. None of
this is true, however, of the steps taken for a Tiv girl at puberty, the
most important of which is scarification. The process has been
charmingly described by Akiga Sai, a gifted and articulate Tiv
leader, using as examples the fictitious characters of Agabi, the artist,
Ayawer, the mother, and Ahobee, the young girl.

> Ayawer: Agabi, I am bringing my daughter to-morrow to have
> the body-markings done. Although she has quite reached puberty,
> her stomach is unmarked.
> Agabi: All right, come along to-morrow and I'll do her.

*   *   *

> Ayawer: Come out, Agabi. I've brought my little girl that I came
> to see you about yesterday.
> Agabi: Come, come, Ayawer. Won't you sit down and just let me
> fill a pipe for you? Then when you have had a smoke, we'll get
> down to the marking.
> Ayawer: No, no. Better do it while it is early, before the blood
> begins to circulate.
> Agabi goes and sits down on the ground, takes a razor and makes
> the incisions. He cuts three circles round the navel, and a vertical
> line to the chest which is continued right on up to the neck. For-
> merly, that was all; marks were not made all over the stomach. But
> afterwards, with the introduction of new fashions, other lines were
> made branching out to either side of the woman's body and down-
> wards, in addition to those drawn round the navel. And later on
> there were added still further decorations.
> When Agabi has finished making the incisions, he pours some
> water over them and washes away all the blood. Then he takes the
> charcoal, which he has previously ground up, and rubs it on. Aho-
> bee gets up and goes off. She leaves it for about two days, and then,
> when the cuts have festered, Ayawer looks for a man of good blood
> to come and bathe them ... [They are dressed with palm oil and
> powdered camwood until they heal.] When all is quite finished, the
> young man who is courting her kills a chicken for her, and Ahobee
> can go and make fun of the girls who have not been marked.[3]

Is this a ritual? The Tiv do not seem to think so. According to
Akiga, the traditional reason for having these scars made is so that the
skin on a woman's belly will be drawn tight and not become flabby,
"like that of the foreign women."[4] The Tiv insist that the purpose of
the scars is to make themselves more attractive.[5] The first British colo-

nial officer to comment on the "stomachic decorations" reported that "they are apparently of ornamental significance only," and all Western authorities have shared his opinion.[6] The express point of this ornamentation is to give aesthetic satisfaction to one's lover, and the erotic element is frequently made clear in a pun: the scar patterns are called *idiar*, "sexual desire," rather than by their proper name *ndiar*, "mudfish."[7] The scars are also said to make a girl's belly tender and erogenous, and "a woman who has them will demand more sexual attention."[8]

There is thus little evidence to support a view of Tiv scarification as an initiatory rite. The application of the scars is almost perfunctory, endowed with no sacral aura, and anyone may watch.[9] No special preparations are made, and no special rules govern either the girl's behavior or that of the artist who cuts the scars. Although it is true that the northern Tiv occasionally refer to scarification as "the circumcision of women,"[10] this does not establish it as an initiation, for the Tiv say that circumcision too has no religious motivation. The only reason given for the performance of circumcision is that Tiv women find the prepuce repugnant, and will not think of entering into sexual relations with a man who has not been circumcised. Once again, the purpose of the operation seems to be aesthetic and pragmatic-erotic, if native informants are to be believed.[11]

There are, however, any number of reasons why such statements need not be the last word on the subject. Deeper meanings of any religious datum may be forgotten, as is apparently the case with the most solemn Tiv invocation: "The moon is a maiden; the sun, a manchild," for which Tiv can offer no explanation.[12] Informants may also deliberately conceal information they consider sacred, and we must remember that no one who has studied the Tiv was initiated into their secret cults.[13] Akiga makes a pointed warning to those who would gather information: "If you wish to ask [the elders] about something, and do not go about it in the right way, you will never get the truth from them. They will think that you have been sent by the white man, and give you no information of any value."[14] Finally, it is possible that the ritual significance of an act is so generally understood that it is rarely made explicit. Such is the case with our handshake and with most unconscious rituals. Tiv scarification may well fall into the same category.

If it is an unconscious ritual, however, how can we possibly hope to understand it without the benefit of informants' glosses? Although the method has its risks, one may perhaps learn something by considering the scars themselves, for one basic pattern is applied to the belly of every Tiv woman. Further, the Tiv names that denote the constituent elements of that pattern prove helpful in its interpretation. In order to appreciate this, however, it is first necessary to examine a number of Tiv ideas, particularly those regarding genealogy, the land (*tar*), and the sacred objects (*Akombo*).

Traditionally the Tiv regarded themselves as descendants of one eponymous ancestor, Tiv, who lived some fourteen to seventeen generations before the present time.[15] European contact caused this opinion to be revised, since the whites obviously did not descend from Tiv; accordingly, an earlier generation was added. Adam and Ifé became the primordial ancestors of all humanity and Tiv their most important son, Europeans being descended from one of their other children.[16] Certain basic principles remain despite this change of detail: the underlying unity of humanity is affirmed, and genealogy is regarded as the means of assessing the ties that bind people to one another. A fundamental tenet of this system is that the more closely related two people are—that is, the fewer generations back a common ancestor is located—the closer is the social bond that ties them together in everyday life. Conversely, the more distant their relations, the cooler their normal dealings, if dealings there be. The genealogical argument thus clearly explains the difficulties that exist between Tiv and Europeans, to give just one practical example of the system's logic.[17]

Genealogy has thus been called "the key to Tiv social organization,"[18] and each Tiv must possess extensive knowledge of his own genealogy and those of the others with whom he comes in contact. Such knowledge allows him to determine whom he may marry, what his territorial rights are, whom he may count on for assistance, who may bewitch him, and who will protect him against witchcraft. In the recent past, his genealogy also governed where he could travel safely and where he could expect to meet danger.[19] The importance of genealogies in all dealings is so great that they are constantly discussed, debated, and cited as evidence in any dispute. Specific details are always being contested, revised, and even forgotten, but none of this changes the central importance of genealogy to the Tiv. As Laura Bohannan put it:

> The first article of Tiv belief is that there *is* a genealogy; that all Tiv are children of Tiv through a known and knowable line of descent. The substance of this genealogy is debatable and debated. What one may not question is its existence, its relevance to present life, and its nature—that is, as a record of the past existence of living human beings whose names are remembered in the genealogy. It is difficult—and in some cases impossible—for Tiv to comprehend that this belief *can* be questioned. Socially and culturally,

their concepts and values are based on this belief and permeated by it. One may question any given man's knowledge of the genealogy, or any part of it; one may not question that there is a *true* genealogy and that it is both known—by someone, somewhere—and knowable.[20]

Genealogy also determines patterns of dwelling and land usage in very definite ways. Residence is patrilocal, and almost 90 percent of all the men in any of the territorial segments the Tiv call *tar* (plural *utar*) consider themselves to be descendants of a common patrilineal ancestor. Collectively, all the inhabitants of a given tar are referred to by their ancestor's name, being called "those of *X,*" and—a striking fact—the tar they inhabit is called "those of *X*" as well, the land and its people being seen as an inseparable unity.[21]

There is no set size for a tar; indeed, with each successive generation the tar is expected to grow, along with its population, barring some catastrophe.[22] Each minimal tar belongs to a series of ever larger utar, culminating in the largest tar which is descended from the most distant ancestor, Tiv, and called accordingly *TarTiv,* "the land of the descendants of Tiv," or "Tivland" as it is regularly translated.[23] The principle along which utar recombine to form ever larger utar is once again genealogical. The founding ancestors of any two adjacent utar are always said to have been brothers, their father being the founding ancestor of their combined territory. This process may be repeated back through all seventeen generations of world history, and the result is always the same: a diagram of the genealogical tree is the same as a map of the geographic territory (see Figure 8).

One ramification of this set of ideas is that it is impossible for Tiv to conceive of a tar without people. The two are inevitably associated, and Paul Bohannan defined tar as "a territory associated with and defined by a social group."[24] A Tiv elder expressed it better, however, when he distinguished the tar from the earth or soil (*nya*), saying, "Plants grow in the earth, but come up on the tar. *Plants and people and their compounds comprise the tar.*"[25] Included in this statement is a view of the tar as productive, fertile, supporting the life of its people through the crops it brings forth. Indeed, the Tiv expression for a state of prosperity, well-being, and satisfaction is *ya tar,* which means "eating the tar."[26]

The tar is intrinsically good, and well-being is therefore the natural state of affairs. It is possible, however, to "spoil the land" (*vihi tar*) through ill will, aggression, conflict among the family group, or any number of ritual transgressions against the sacred objects known as *Akombo*. An Akombo can be almost anything—a mound of earth, a special type of grass, a decorated ancestral skull. Most literally, the

Akombo are the physical objects themselves, each of which is said to control a certain sphere of existence: childbirth, hunting, disease, the crops, and so forth. More broadly, they have been said to *be* these spheres of existence, and they may also be seen as the sacred power that lies behind the physical objects and allows them to control activity within these areas of life. According to tradition, at the time of

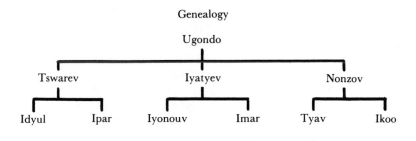

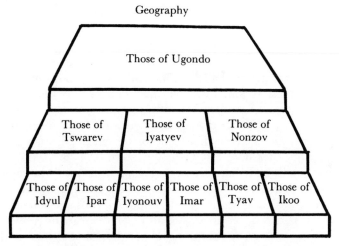

Figure 8. Genealogy and geography. The genealogy given here is an actual one, taken from Abraham, *The Tiv People*, p. 103. Below is a hypothetical schematic rendition of what the living arrangements ought to be for the descendants of the individuals named in the genealogy. Those descended from brothers (for example, Idyul and Ipar) ought to inhabit neighboring utar (referred to as "those of Idyul" and "those of Ipar"), which may be viewed together as a broader territorial unit originating with and descending from the father of those brothers (here, Tswarev) and referred to by his name ("those of Tswarev"). In this way, the map of the land effectively conforms to and reproduces the map of the lineage as charted in a family tree.

creation the Tiv were given knowledge of ritual and the magico-religious power known as *Tsav*, both of which are necessary for the proper use of Akombo. When the Akombo are properly maintained by one who possesses sufficient Tsav, they preserve welfare within their sphere of influence.[27]

Although there are hundreds of Akombo and more are constantly being adopted from other tribes, they can be divided roughly into two classes called the small and great Akombo.[28] Small Akombo tend to be privately owned and have a relatively narrow range of effects and powers, whereas the great Akombo are usually held in trust by a secret cult group of learned elders, the *Mba Tsav* ("Those of Power"), and secure the well-being of the entire tar.

Each Akombo carries with it certain ritual prohibitions, and to trespass these is to make oneself vulnerable to its power. In the case of the small Akombo, this power turns against the offender, "seizing" him and making him ill. He must seek out the master of the violated Akombo, who—if properly approached and persuaded—will "repair" (*sor*) the Akombo, thus setting the offense right, returning the Akombo to its normal benevolence, and restoring the offender's health. Such "repairing" is normally done by pouring the blood of a sacrificed animal, usually a chicken, over the Akombo so as to propitiate or revitalize it, and then dripping some of the blood onto the right hand of the trespasser in order to bring him back into proper relations with the restored Akombo.[29]

With regard to the great Akombo there are a few important differences. First, an offense against one of the great Akombo does not harm the offender alone but disrupts the well-being of the entire community, "spoiling the tar." Second, it is the Mba Tsav who repair the great Akombo, rather than a private owner. Third, a higher order of sacrifice is needed to restore the Akombo to its original state. Human sacrifice is said to be required, and although there are no proven cases of this on record, grisly tales of ritual murder, "flesh debts," and nocturnal cannibalistic feasts abound.[30] Finally, it is not sufficient to repair the great Akombo only when they have been offended; the Mba Tsav hold rituals for them on a regular basis in order to prevent any attrition of their power.

Everything the Mba Tsav do is cloaked in secrecy, a fact that leads to their being regarded as both ghoulish sorcerers and national saviors by other Tiv, who know of their doings chiefly by rumor. Among other means, the Mba Tsav screen their activity from public scrutiny by using a "secret language," which substitutes one noun for every other in normal speech. One such substitution is particularly important for any study of Tiv religion: one of the great Akombo, regarded

Figure 9. Bone Imborivungu. This piece has been embellished with a model of a woman's head, pebbles at both ends of the bone to attach the head and to form a base respectively, and—most significantly for our purposes—the inscription of concentric circles around the navel and vertical lines in a diamond pattern running from one end of the bone to the other through the navel. This pattern thus closely parallels that of women's scarification. Based on a photograph in Abraham, *The Tiv People,* plate 3.

by the majority of scholars as the most important of them all, is called the *tar,* and performing its ritual is called "repairing the tar" (*sorun tar*).[31]

This sacred object is the *Imborivungu,* or "owl-pipe," which is traditionally made from a human tibia that has been carved and decorated and has had a hole bored in its center; in this century the Imborivungu is cast in brass on occasion, but still retains its traditional form (see Figures 9–12). A myth recorded by Abraham recounts the origin of the Imborivungu, tracing its invention to the children of Tiv: Poor, Chongo, and Pusu.

> According to this legend Poor died leaving no issue, and his brothers Chongo and Pusu who survived him took one of his bones to keep his memory fresh; they placed it in a lidded basket, forbidding any but themselves to look upon it under pain of death and said that if this rule were broken, the fertility of the crops would suffer and the whole of the Tiv perish. To enhance the efficacy of this bone, whenever a woman had a miscarriage the blood was poured over it; later, however, this bone was destroyed in a fire and the successors of the brothers substituted two other human bones for it.[32]

Figure 10. Bone Imborivungu. Note the addition of cowrie shells, common symbols of female fertility due to their vulvular shape, to represent the woman's eyes. Based on a photograph in Abraham, *The Tiv People*, plate 2.

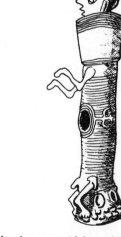

Figure 11. Brass Imborivungu. Although the properties of brass allow new elaborations of form (as, for instance, the addition of hands and feet here), most details of the bone Imborivungu have been retained (for example, the lumps at the base where previously pebbles were found). Three concentric rings surround the navel, and branch out to either side to form the wings proper to the "swallow" pattern of women's scarification. Based on a photograph in Balfour, "Ritual and Secular Uses of Vibrating Membranes as Voice Disguisers," p. 54.

Figure 12. Brass Imborivungu. Reliance on bone models is less evident in this example than in Figure 11, with the result that the idea of the Imborivungu as a statue of a woman is stressed more fully. Female fertility is also emphasized by the use of cowrie-shell shapes in place of the abstract scarification lines descending from throat to navel. The concentric circles around the navel are quite prominent, and may represent sheaves of grain. Based on a photograph in Balfour, "Ritual and Secular Uses of Vibrating Membranes as Voice Disguisers," p. 54.

A number of points are worth stressing here. First the Imborivungu is a relic of the primordial ancestors, and as such constitutes a link between the living and the dead, between the present and the beginning of time.[33] Second, it is kept as an esoteric mystery, hidden from the view of all but a select few. Third, the fertility of the land and the well-being of all the Tiv depend upon it. Fourth, it is periodically repaired with the blood of a miscarriage—which is to say, with life that might have been. Finally, the myth charters the establishment of new Imborivungu when old ones are destroyed, wear out, or disappear.

Reports vary somewhat as to the rites performed to repair the Imborivungu by the Mba Tsav. According to most, sacrificial blood is poured into the Imborivungu through its central hole (the account cited below is atypical in this regard) and then is scattered on fields and dripped into wells.[34] There is general agreement that human blood is required, and some sources specify that this must be blood derived from a miscarriage or an abortion, as in the myth cited above.[35] Akiga further specifies that it must be an abortion obtained from a woman who has not had any children previously—that is, her fertility must exist as a state of sheer potentiality which is fully concentrated in the fetus given to the Imborivungu.[36] The most graphic account is probably that given by Abraham:

> This consecration [the annual repair of the Imborivungu] is effected with the blood of an abortion but . . . a natural abortion is unacceptable and an abortion must be brought about deliberately [by drugs secretly administered to a pregnant woman].
>
> Abortion is caused once only to the same woman, but it is not in any way essential that the woman should be the wife of one of the *Mba Tsav;* the essential thing is to obtain blood from the abortion and pour it over the *Imborivungu.* A woman who has been so treated is specially favored by God, and it is considered that she will become pregnant again immediately and be the mother of sound offspring.
>
> The foetus is taken and the ears, feet, hands, nose, and liver are cooked in a pot; little fragments of flesh are then pinched off and scattered about with the words "The sun is a boy; the moon is a girl." The initiates present then wash their hands in the liquid in which the parts have been cooked, and the *Imborivungu* is also immersed in it; it is then taken and drops shaken off it on to the fields and into the wells. The navel string is kept and every year or so it is immersed in water and this water is sprinkled over the farms and into the wells by means of the *Imborivungu.*[37]

Whether such grisly practices ever took place is almost impossible to tell. One recalls Akiga's warning of the deliberate deception practiced by Tiv elders upon inquiring whites ("Especially is this so in the case of one whom they know to be in the government service"), and wonders if Captain Abraham's leg was not being pulled a bit.[38] But other authorities give reports that are extremely similar, including Akiga himself. One can only conclude that if deception has been practiced, it has been practiced upon the Tiv as well as the whites. Whether or not these rites were ever performed, the bulk of the Tiv believe that they are carried out regularly: at the level of ideology, at least, they are very real indeed.[39]

If we cannot ascertain the physical reality of these rites, it is nevertheless possible to make sense of their symbolism, which remains the same whether the actions were performed or only imagined. By the sacrifice of a life *in potentio,* it is clear that the life of the Imborivungu—of the tar, in Mba Tsav terms—is renewed so that all may prosper.[40] The steps taken after the Imborivungu has received this offering are also highly significant. The liquid that contains the fetus is shaken from the Imborivungu onto the fields and wells, an act for which Akiga offers the following explanation: "Thus the crops of the whole group will be good, and the first woman to draw water from the well the next morning will straightway conceive and bear a son, even though she had hitherto been barren."[41] The goal of the rite is thus fertility in its twin aspects—"bumper crops and a high birth rate," as the Bohannans put it.[42]

Abraham's account also specifies that the libation to fields and wells is repeated annually with the water in which the fetus' umbilical cord has been preserved. The umbilical cord, of course, is the means whereby a mother nourishes and sustains the life she is preparing within her, and is the most intimate connection between mother and child. Little has been written on Tiv notions of physiology, but from certain details it appears that they believe the cord to run from the navel of the mother to that of the child. Thus, in the many rites performed for the pregnant woman, offerings of blood, earth, or the excreta of sacrificial animals are regularly placed on the woman's navel to nourish her and her child *in utero*.[43] Interestingly enough, this is similar to the way in which offerings are made to the Imborivungu, libations being poured through its central hole or "navel."

This fact brings us to another aspect of Imborivungu symbolism. For if the object is both a relic of the ancestors and the mystic embodiment of the tar, it is also a woman, ever ready to bring forth new life. Examination of numerous Imborivungu shows that they are always carved and decorated to be statues of human figures, and almost invariably statues of women.[44] What is more, the Imborivungu are often given a set of abdominal markings roughly identical to the scarifications produced on women at puberty (compare Figures 9–12 with Figures 13–16).

With this realization, we are brought back to the scarification pattern. As Akiga stated, the essential marks cut on each girl are three concentric circles around the navel, and a vertical line running from the throat to the navel. More lines may be added over the course of a lifetime, but these four scars constitute the basic framework and starting point for all elaboration. According to Akiga, in the past no other marks were made: lines and circles were enough.[45]

Has this design some deeper meaning? Consideration of Tiv terminology regarding lines and circles leads to such a hypothesis, for two crucial terms are not limited to geometrical usage but have a much broader range of meanings. The first of these is *nongo,* "line" or "row." Nongo can be used to indicate any straight line: a hoed-up ridge on which crops are planted, a queue in which people wait, or a line

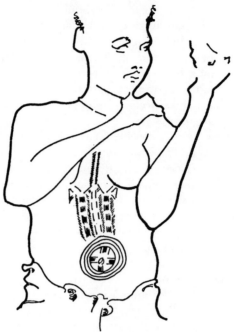

Figure 13. Women's scarification, "mudfish" pattern. The scarification of each woman begins with one or two lines that descend from the throat to the navel, where they join a set of two or three concentric circles around the navel. This basic design is then elaborated throughout a woman's life. If no horizontal lines have been added to each side of the navel, the pattern is called a "mudfish." Based on a photograph in Ottenberg and Ottenberg, *Cultures and Societies in Africa,* following p. 182.

drawn upon the ground. By extension, it can be used to refer to one's genealogical lineage or a segment within a more extensive lineage.[46] In this context it denotes the derivation of society from the past, stretching from any given individual of the present back through his ancestors to Tiv himself. The nongo is one's family and heritage, one's land and traditions—all that has been passed down through time, as well as the series of ancestors who have preserved these gifts and handed them one to another.

The second significant term is *kwav* (singular *kwagh*), "concentric circles." Most literally, the word *kwav* refers to the concentric rings used to construct the conical roofs of Tiv houses, and it is applied by analogy to the age-sets that are formed every three years of all the men roughly eighteen to twenty years old.[47] In contrast to numerous

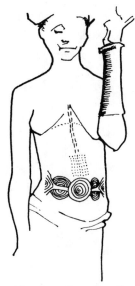

Figure 14. Women's scarification, "swallow" pattern. The addition of horizontal lines across the abdomen to either side of the navel changes the "mudfish" pattern to a "swallow," the excrescences being interpreted as wings. In origin, the two patterns are identical, however, being based upon the throat-navel lines and the concentric circles surrounding the navel. Based on a photograph in East, *Akiga's Story*, following p. 176.

other Bantu tribes, the Tiv do not reckon history in terms of their age-sets; the past is mentioned only in the context of genealogies or myths.[48] Rather, like ripples on a pond, the kwav spread gradually into the future as members of each kwagh age together and are replaced by other kwav.[49]

If nongo represents past and kwav future, the present is also found within the scarification design in the form of the woman's navel. Standing at the center of the pattern, her navel is the axis on which the pattern turns: nongo ends there, and kwav begin, just as the lineage of the past produced this woman, who will in turn produce the age-sets of the future from out of her own belly. Her navel, the point of nurturance for future generations, is paradoxically both part of the scarification pattern and not part of it, as it is her own from birth and does not have to be added artificially. At puberty, however, it takes on new significance as the vital center where life will be formed, and at that moment it becomes the center and starting point for the symbolic design that makes a girl into a woman.

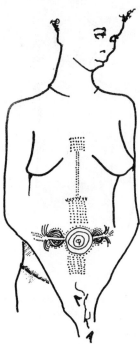

Figure 15. Women's scarification, "swallow" pattern. Based on a photograph in Rowe, "Abdominal Cicatrisation of the Munshi Tribe, Nigeria," p. 179. (Munshi is a name used for the Tiv in some of the older literature.)

The scarification pattern may thus represent something a good deal more profound than a "mudfish" or a "swallow," despite the fact that these are the interpretations Tiv regularly offer.[50] At the most abstract level, the line and circles of the pattern may represent the structure of time, placing the pubescent girl at the intersection of past and future. Beyond that, it may be taken as a picture of the process of genealogical descent, whereby she is shown to be heir of the ancestors, bearer of descendants, and guarantor of the lineage's continuity. Given the intimate connection between the lineage and the land, the pattern might also be taken to represent the tar as well, which is also inherited through the nongo and expected to expand with the kwav.[51]

It is not enough to see this pattern as merely a didactic device whereby important Tiv concepts are prominently displayed. Rather, its effect is transformative: it is the means whereby a girl becomes a woman, and the mark of this transformation is the girl's laughter at her former companions who have not yet been scarified.[52] The scars are said to promote fertility,[53] most obviously in terms of the genera-

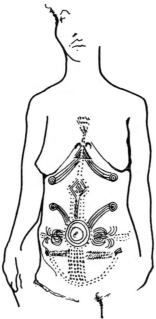

Figure 16. Women's scarification, "swallow" pattern. This is an extremely elaborate example, probably the product of years of operations. Based on a photograph in Rowe, "Abdominal Cicatrisation of the Munshi Tribe, Nigeria," p. 179.

tion of human life but also in terms of agriculture, for among the Tiv, adult women bear responsibility for the crops. Ownership of the land and granaries is in their hands, they do most of the agricultural labor, and they possess the bulk of the tribe's agricultural knowledge.[54]

In a very concrete sense, responsibility for the fertility of people and crops thus devolves upon Tiv women when they receive their scars. Within the esoteric wisdom of the Mba Tsav, responsibility for these twin aspects of fertility is said to rest with the great Akombo, most particularly the Imborivungu, which is referred to as the tar, the land. And, as we have seen, the Imborivungu is but a mirror image of each adult female. It too is a woman, and it too bears the same scars.

One might even go so far as to argue that scarification makes every woman into an Akombo, makes every woman into the Imborivungu, makes every woman into the tar. Four lines cut at puberty make a woman the guardian of fertility and well-being, heir of the past and creator of the future. The scars themselves are simultaneously the means of her transformation and the visible mark that this transformation has been completed, making each girl a woman and a sacred object for all to see.

5

Festa
das Moças
Novas:
The Cosmic
Tour

Among the Tukuna of the Northwest Amazon the ceremony performed for girls at menarche is one of the most spectacular initiations
practiced in South America.[1] Preparations for the festival may take
three months or longer, during which time the initiand or *vorëki,* as
she is called, is kept in seclusion, waiting for the climactic three days
and nights, when three hundred or more participants gather for con-
tinuous drinking, feasting, and dancing. Many of these guests, particularly the men, wear eerie and dramatic bark-cloth masks and costumes to represent demonic beings.[2] Enormous trumpets and
megaphones sound nightly, and other musical instruments of various
types contribute to the din. The Festa das Moças Novas ("Festival of
the New Maiden") or *vorëki cheii* ("Drink of the Initiand") is the most
important Tukuna ritual, there being no other major ceremonies to
rival it, nor any significant male initiation.[3]

The Tukuna ceremony differs from the other examples we have
considered in that it is not rooted in an agricultural society. Although
agricultural products are an important part of the Tukuna diet, and
much labor—particularly women's labor—is devoted to the cultiva-
tion of such plants as bitter and sweet manioc, corn, and yams, the
chief subsistence activity is fishing, and fish are the principal Tukuna
food.[4]

This socioeconomic difference implies a profound difference in religious world view, particularly with regard to the issue of fertility,
which is usually a major focus of women's initiatory rites. Agricultural peoples usually sense a parallelism or harmony between their
two categories of fertility—human and botanical—desiring growth
and abundance in both. Increased population results in more workers

in the fields, more land cleared, more seeds planted, more crops reaped. More crops mean more food and the ability to sustain a greater population. Hunters and fishers, in contrast, regard their world quite differently: they usually sense conflict or competition between their two categories of fertility (human and animal). To them, an increase in human population constitutes a threat to the population of the game. There will be more killings at first, then fewer animals left to reproduce, fewer killings in the long run, less food, and general hardship. Conversely, an oversupply of animals threatens to overrun human dwellings and culture completely, returning them to the virgin jungle. Thus, whereas agriculturalists tend to desire increase in all realms of nature, hunters and fishers favor the preservation of a delicate balance, a stable ecosystem without the possibility of dramatic growth. Human fertility is regarded ambivalently: although necessary and desirable in moderation, it becomes destructive when carried to the extreme. This attitude colors the religion of hunters and fishers deeply, and explains important aspects of Tukuna initiation.[5]

The Tukuna divide their world into a number of planes and realms. In addition to the earth's surface, there are several underworlds. One, Nëchaku, is the place where maize first grew, whence it was taken by Ariana, a heroine of primordial times; little more is told of it.[6] More important is Nāpi̧, an underworld connected to the earth by caves, and in which dwell the most ancient of all beings: demons called Noo, who are extremely threatening to human beings.[7] A separate part of Nāpi̧ is the subaquatic area in which dwells another class of demons, the Dyëvaë, giant serpent or catfish who control the river currents and the yields of fish.[8]

These are the realms that lie beneath; above, there are others. Several heavens are envisioned: one in which live people much like terrestrial humans; one inhabited by the goddess Ta-ë who rules over souls of the dead; and one (the existence of which is debated) where the king vultures, loftiest of birds, are found. Far beyond these heavens lies the realm of the sun, moon, and stars.[9]

Such is the Tukuna map of the universe as reported by Curt Nimuendaju, a pioneering ethnologist of the first order. Yet for all the precision and clarity of his reporting, Nimuendaju seems inconsistent on one crucial point of the Tukuna cosmology. He asserts: "It is manifestly impossible for a living person to enter heaven; not even a shaman can do so while dreaming. Hence, knowledge of things there is confined to the experiences of the few human beings who, carried up by celestial girls wishing to marry them, later returned."[10] The contradiction is inescapable: first he says no one may enter heaven, then he says some have done so. Even if we were to accept only the latter,

less restrictive half of the statement, it would seem that only young
men can enter the upper realms, and that, too, is expressly contra-
dicted by a number of myths in which young girls are said to have
ascended to the heavens, usually by donning feathers or by being
transformed into birds.[11] Perhaps the most interesting is the myth of
Ariana:

> There was a little girl who had been an orphan since her infancy.
> The uncle and his wife with whom she lived did not like her. She
> walked alone along a jungle path and wept. Ta-ë came to her, but
> the little one did not recognize her. "Why do you cry?" asked Ta-ë.
> "Mother," answered the little girl, "my uncle does not like me and
> treats me very badly!" "Come to my arms!" said Ta-ë. She em-
> braced the little one, and without the child's noticing anything
> they ascended to heaven. She washed the little girl, gave her the
> name of Ariana, and reared her.
>
> Ariana became a very pretty woman. Many men of the celestial
> people desired her, and she had love affairs with many of them; but
> because of this she also had many enemies, some of whom invited
> her one day for a stroll. They went with her to where the upper
> world ends, where they suddenly transformed themselves into
> toads, hopped in all directions, and disappeared, leaving Ariana
> alone.
>
> Ariana took the shape of a swallow and flew up to the Sun. Fly-
> ing just above him, she plucked out a lock of red hair and one of
> blue hair. With these Ariana attempted to decorate her armbands,
> which would make her even prettier and irresistible. The Sun, how-
> ever, exasperated at her audacity, fetched her such a kick that she
> went flying through heaven and earth, finally stopping in the un-
> derworld called Nëchaku. When she returned from there, she
> brought maize for the inhabitants of the earth.[12]

Ariana succeeds in traversing all the cosmic realms, and as a result
of her travels she wins a gift of inestimable value for mankind. From
earth she ascends to the heavens, and beyond them to the sun. From
the sun she descends to the underworlds, and from them back to
earth, bringing corn with her. The myth recounts something similar
to the experiences of a young woman at initiation, who also succeeds
in traversing the cosmic realms and winning gifts of enormous value.

This parallelism is expressed in many ways. The initiand is believed susceptible to all varieties of supernatural power during the
time of her initiation. She is said to be assaulted by demons, particularly the Noo, and the slightest breach of ritual precautions will permit them to kill her, suck the viscera from her body, and carry her
empty body to their domain.[13] It is also a time when celestial beings
may appear to the girl, bringing her advice, knowledge, solace, and

even carrying her up to the home of the immortals.[14] This tradition of immortals appearing to the young at puberty has played a crucial part in Tukuna messianic movements, almost all of which began with a vision experienced by a pubescent girl or boy. In such visions, immortals appear and give the girl or boy instructions for the assistance of their people. Standing at the threshold between childhood and adulthood, the young are thought to be receptive to the supernatural presence, and the supernatural realms are particularly accessible to them.[15]

This same ideology is also expressed in the symbolism of the chamber in which the vorëki is secluded. This chamber is constructed for the occasion inside the large family dwelling (*maloca*). It is circular and very small, not more than two meters in diameter, made of palm leaves lashed together, and set against the eastern or western wall of the maloca, depending on the moiety to which the initiand belongs. The only furnishing is a hammock in which the vorëki sleeps during her isolation.

In the past, anthropologists considered this chamber to be something of a defensive perimeter, a wall that protected the initiand from the demonic Noo who threatened her safety at all times,[16] but more recent research has forced a change from that interpretation. One suggestive piece of evidence is an etymology advanced by Otto Zerries, who has argued that the name given the seclusion chamber, $napi^n i^n$, is made up of elements meaning "to go" (i^n with initial nasalization, thus $^n i^n$) and "into the underworld (Nāpi)."[17] Rather than a protection from the Noo, the chamber is a place where one actively enters their realm and courts their dangers. The period of seclusion is nothing less than a descent into the underworld.

This descent is only one of the cosmic journeys required of the initiand. A celestial ascent is also necessary, as is again shown in the symbolism of the chamber. On the outside of its walls symbolic designs are painted, examples of which are given in Figure 17. A fair amount of variation is permitted in the execution of these designs and numerous emblems appear, including such recent innovations as a watch and a steel ax.[18] The presence of four specific designs is mandatory, however, and three of these are images of the celestial realm beyond the heavens: sun, moon, and star.[19] The point is clear: when the girl exits from the underworld, she enters a totally different realm, the realm of the above.

The significance of the fourth required emblem is somewhat different. The picture is of a deer, generally explained as the Tukuna symbol of vigilance and thus a visual reminder for all those present to watch over the initiand.[20] This may well be so, but it is also helpful to

Figure 17. The seclusion hut $(na\text{-}pi^n i^n)$. The designs painted on the outside wall of the hut represent the sun (upper left), moon (crescent, upper right), and a star (upper right). A fourth design, that of a deer, is said to be mandatory but does not appear in this example, unless it is represented by the highly stylized figure in the lower left. A fish appears here in the lower right, but is not a regular feature of most seclusion hut designs. Based on a photograph in Hanke, *Völkerkundliche Forschungen in Südamerika,* facing p. 108.

recall the peculiar role assigned the deer in Tukuna mythology. In one myth it was the deer that brought the seeds of all cultivated plants except maize to man.[21] In another it is told that "in ancient times the deer was a man-eating jaguar. In order to stop his depredations, Dyoi [the culture hero] gave him a punch under the jaw that knocked the ascending rami [vertical ends of the lower jawbone] through the top of his skull, where they appeared as antlers. Since then, the deer has been inoffensive."[22] In both instances the deer undergoes a transition from a wild, uncivilized state to one of peace, well-being, and productivity. In structuralist terms, it is a change from nature to culture, or, to employ a different vocabulary, from chaos to cosmos or immaturity to maturity. This is precisely the transition made by the initiand. The seclusion chamber is, in truth, something of a retort or crucible, in which a dramatic transformation is effected. The Tukuna use a preindustrial metaphor to describe its workings in a song that is sung shortly after the girl emerges from her isolation:

Oh, what is it now that our vorëki has come among us, all covered with plumage?
Oh, what dost thou say now of her toucan feathers?
Like a caterpillar [in chrysalis] our vorëki was placed in seclusion by us![23]

The chamber is thus compared to a cocoon, into which the girl went as a caterpillar, immature, plain, and terrestrial, and from which she emerges a butterfly, mature, beautiful, and celestial.

The ritual begins when a girl notices her first menstrual bleeding. She removes all the necklaces and ornaments she normally wears, and hangs them on a crossbeam in her family's maloca, where they will readily be found by her mother. She then retreats into the nearby forest and hides. When her mother discovers the ornaments, she searches for her daughter, who assists her in this by tapping two small sticks together and producing a regular, rhythmic call. Once found, the girl is brought back to the maloca and placed within the seclusion chamber, which is especially erected for the occasion. There she remains, cut off from contact with all except her mother and her father's sister, while preparations are made for the culminating feast.

During this time of seclusion the vorëki is thought to be in the underworld itself, and as such is surrounded by invisible Noo who threaten her life.[24] This danger becomes most acute toward the end of her seclusion as the Moça Nova festival gets underway. This celebration, the culmination of each girl's initiation, usually lasts three days and nights and must begin with a new or full moon—times of change and new beginnings.[25]

Preparations for the Moça Nova include the production of vast quantities of intoxicating drinks and the procurement of much smoked meat and fish. A corral is also erected outside the maloca, adjoining the vorëki's seclusion chamber. Here sacred, secret musical instruments are played each night, and a cleared path leads from the corral to the river, where the instruments are hidden by day.

For the first two days guests arrive by canoe, often coming from a great distance. They are greeted with drink by the initiand's father's brother, who is officially in charge of the ceremony in accord with Tukuna patrilineal ideology. Many begin dancing and making music with a number of secular instruments, the most important of which are turtleshell drums, bamboo horns, and stamping tubes.[26] This music, highly rhythmic in nature, continues throughout the celebration, and any slackening of the beat is expected to increase the danger that threatens the initiand from the assaulting Noo.[27]

If this constant rhythmic music does have an apotropaic function, however, it meets its counterpoint in the eerie tones of the two wind instruments collectively called *uaricana*, which are believed to be nothing less than the voice of the Noo themselves.[28] These uaricana appear in two varieties: paxiuba wood megaphones that are six and a half meters long and horns that are four to six meters long, the latter being made of bark rolled into cylinders. Women are forbidden to see the uaricana on pain of death, and they are among the most sacred items of the Tukuna world.[29]

These massive instruments produce an eldritch sound, truly unearthly, and they have been described as the "acoustic presence" of the spirits.[30] The spirits are also visually present in the equally unearthly bark-cloth masks and costumes worn by many of the guests. A number of different demons may be represented, but most common are Oma, the spirit of the wind, equipped with a phallus half a meter long; Yurupari, the "devil"; Uaiuari, a monstrous ape; Bëru, a female butterfly with elongated breasts, perhaps responsible for the origin of disease; Machi, the jaguar; Chavi, the maize, and many others (see Figures 18–21).[31] A detailed myth tells of the origin of these masks. The story begins with a journey made by a group of Tukuna to visit some countrymen. In the middle of their trip, they found a shelter and stopped to spend the night.

> While they were camped there, a woman of the group gave birth; because of this event they resolved to remain a few days until she was in condition to accompany them farther. They went out to hunt, but found nothing and had to sleep hungry. In the darkness of the night they heard a gnawing sound. They surrounded and killed the rodent, which was an enormous paca.
>
> All except the parturient and her husband ate of the meat, and on the following day they went out to hunt again, leaving the woman and her little child alone in the shelter. Suddenly she saw a Noo in human shape approach, saying that the paca had been his son, whosse death he came to avenge. At midnight the Noo would come, blowing a snailshell trumpet; those who had not eaten of the paca's flesh must climb a certain species of tree, peeling the bark behind them.[32]

This information proved to be true, and that night the Noo attacked, blowing their trumpets as promised. Unable to wake any of her companions other than her husband, the woman led him up the tree, carrying her infant along, and from that vantage point they heard the screams of the others as they were killed by the Noo. The next

Figure 18. Oma, the spirit of the wind. The red horizontal lines across the face of this mask indicate that the demon portrayed is one of those who ate human flesh. Normally Oma is equipped with an enormous phallus, but this is not visible here, perhaps hidden behind the bark-cloth around the masquerader's torso. For an example in which the phallus is evident, see Nimuendaju, *The Tukuna,* p. 201, although the mask there is much less elaborate in detail. This example is based on a photograph in Zerries, "Die Tanzmasken der Tukuna," table 7, following p. 376.

Figure 19. Masked dancer. This shows a much less elaborate costume than that in Figure 18, and no clear mythic reference is discernible beyond the fact that a demon is represented. The aggressive sexuality of the demon is clearly apparent in his large phallus, and from the dancer's position it seems possible that coital motions are being enacted in his dance. Based on a photograph in Schultz, "Fra i Tucuna dell'alta Amazzonia," p. 146.

morning the woman and her husband returned to their maloca and related what had happened. An expedition was quickly organized for revenge, and following the advice of an old shaman the members of this party went to the cavern of the Noo, barricaded the opening, and built a fire into which they threw a great quantity of hot peppers, driving the resultant fumes into the cavern.

Soon a great racket arose from the interior; the Tukuna yelled inside for those among the Noo who had not eaten human flesh to come out, and thus it happened: there appeared Cherine playing the turtleshell drum, which was his invention, preceded by a few other Noo playing their bamboo horns. These were allowed to depart in peace, and they quickly entered another cavern close by, for another part of the underworld . . .

All the Noo who had eaten human flesh, and whose masks for this reason bear even today a red stripe of urucu in front, died. When the noise within the cavern had ceased, the Tukuna ordered

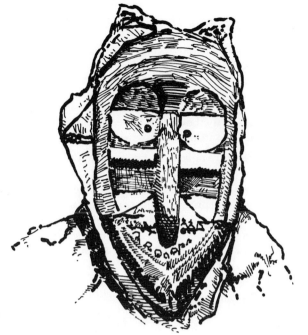

Figure 20. Unidentified mask. Note the emphasis on the jagged teeth, the unnatural asymmetry in the placement of an ear on one side only, the suggestion of horns and a beard, and the horizontal red line that recalls this demon's consumption of human flesh. Based on a photograph in Schultz, "Fra i Tucuna dell'alta Amazzonia," p. 144.

Figure 21. Ape mask, perhaps representing Uaiuari, although he is usually given more specialized facial features. The demonic character is simply but dramatically established by the facial expression, rampant horns or antlers, and the eerie threads strung through the nostrils of the mask. Based on a photograph in Zerries, "Die Tanzmasken der Tukuna," table 5, following p. 372.

one of their servants of the Yagua tribe to enter; he did not return because some of the Noo were still alive and killed him. They again smoked out the cavern, ordering another servant inside to verify the effect. This one walked around the cavern, observing well, and then came out to announce that all the Noo were dead. The Tukuna contemplated the bodies carefully, noting all the details, and later copied the Noo in their costumes.[33]

There are a number of points to be noticed in this myth. First, there is the general theme of revenge upon those who upset the balance of life. Originally, the Tukuna killed and ate the flesh of the paca without having observed the proper hunting rituals and etiquette; as a result, they were made to suffer.[34] Then, those demons who slaughtered the guilty Tukuna were themselves killed for the crime. But in both instances, those who did not take part in the murders (and consumption) were spared from harm.

Among the original Tukuna party, only one family escapes: a young wife, her husband, and their infant child. Of the three, it is the wife who plays the crucial role. She and her husband are saved because she has just given birth, and they are both observing food taboos that forbid them from eating game until their child's umbilical cord falls off.[35] In effect, she and her family are saved first because of her fertility, and second because of their resulting respect for the balance of life. The new human they have produced constitutes a threat to the animal world, and they must not further damage that world by eating meat. Like this woman, the vorëki faces danger from the Noo, which she will have to overcome if she is to attain maturity. The woman of the myth thus provides each initiand with a model for success in overcoming the ancient demons: in order to survive, one must combine (moderate) fertility with a respect for the life of all other species. Only in this way can one avoid unbalancing what Gerardo Reichel-Dolmatoff, following Teilhard de Chardin, has called "the biosphere," thereby provoking violent retribution.[36]

Another point of interest in the myth is the opposition of two types of musical instruments: the trumpets that announce the coming of the hostile spirits, and the turtleshell drums and bamboo horns that announce the peaceful spirits emerging from the cave, those who have never tasted human flesh and who threaten no harm. It is these same instruments that are played outside and inside the maloca respectively, once again with the implications of danger (trumpets) and safety (drums and horns), as we have seen above.

Finally, we come to the express point of the myth: the masks and costumes worn today are faithful reproductions and imitations of the forms the Noo took in mythic times. The masqueraders who don these costumes may thus be said to impersonate or imitate the Noo of old, but this statement is too mild. Rather than just play-acting, the masqueraders actually incarnate the demons, taking on their whole mode of existence from the moment they put on their masks. In costume they race about madly, wielding clubs, breaking things, assaulting the host, guests, the chamber in which the vorëki is secluded, and, once she appears, the vorëki herself.[37] Their actions are impetuous, threatening, and often obscene, a fact that prompted one missionary who observed the ritual to describe their behavior as, "from the point of view of Christian morality, a truly revolting spectacle."[38] It is not enough to say that they act as if they were demons; rather, they abandon their human existence, and for the time they wear the mask they *become* the demons themselves.

Much of the action of the ceremony's first two days and nights is directed toward protecting the initiand from the onslaught of these demons. The girl's family, led by her father's brother, and those guests who are not in costume exercise constant vigilance, and the din of drums, bamboo horns, and stamping tubes is unremitting. The girl herself is painted with black genipa dye from head to toe, a common means of protection against the Noo.[39]

Toward the end of the second day the initiand is decked out in her ceremonial regalia, which is extremely elaborate and beautiful (Figure 22). Her skin, already blackened with genipa dye, is painted with red urucu, onto which hawk plumage is glued. She wears a short cotton tanga or skirt with a wide belt, from which hang strings of glass beads. Glass beads are strung into pectorals and necklaces, and barkcloth tassels and fringe also adorn the vorëki. Two or more strings of these tassels stretch from the girl's neck to hips in front and back, each strip also containing fifteen to twenty spectacular feathers from a toucan's tail, along with white abdominal feathers from the same bird. More toucan feathers are woven into bracelets along with long macaw feathers and bark-cloth fringe, and other plumage is scattered about the costume.[40]

Most spectacular, however, is the headdress that the vorëki wears, made primarily from the brilliant red tail feathers of the macaw, along with a few other feathers from the heron and royal hawk. Feather headgear is encountered with some frequency throughout South America and is usually worn by shamans, who hope to take on the avian mode of being and be assisted in their ecstatic ascent into the heavens.[41] Such an undertaking is possible only for the most accomplished, and the donning of a feather crown carries with it great responsibility.[42] Occasionally such crowns are worn by chiefs, elders, or other men of responsibility, but throughout the continent it is extremely rare for women ever to put on such an ornament.[43]

Figure 22. The vorëki in full regalia. Bracelets, fringe, and tassels, all woven of toucan feathers, are not evident in this example. Note the short skirt and the numerous glass beads, necklaces, and barkcloth tassels. Most significant is the headdress, topped with the brilliant red tail feathers of the macaw. Based in a photograph in Alviano, "Notas etnograficas," facing p. 14.

Beyond this general significance of feather crowns, the crown of red macaw feathers has a very specific meaning among the Tukuna and among many other tribes, particularly those of the Tukanoan language family, in which Tukuna is classified.[44] The Desana, for instance, who regard the macaw as an embodiment of the creative energy of the sun, have a special crown made only of red and yellow feathers which may be worn by none except their priests and which they call *abe bero*, "sun-circle."[45] Similarly, the Koto have a special red feather crown which may be worn only by the heads of families; they call this crown *maa haro*, "feathers of the sun."[46] Tukuna informants state that the sun itself wears a headdress of red macaw feathers, "similar to that used today by a virgin at her puberty festival."[47] The crown is thus a solar diadem, by means of which the initiand partakes of the solar nature and ascends to the sun. The detailed manipulation of this crown during the Moça Nova is of the utmost importance for understanding the ceremony's symbolism.

According to Schultz, great care is taken, even before the vorëki is dressed, that she not be permitted to see the sun.[48] This prohibition also influences her dress, for when the feather crown is placed on her head it is pulled down over her eyes.[49] After she has been dressed, the girl must remain in seclusion until the early morning of the ceremony's third day. At that time her father's brother, his wife, the initiand's mother, and other maternal relatives enter the chamber. Her uncle cuts it open—like a cocoon—and leads the girl out, all of the relatives holding her tightly to protect her from the danger of the Noo, which is greatest at this moment.[50] These relatives dance with the girl until dawn, warding off constant assaults by the masked demons (Figure 23).

Shortly before dawn, the dance swirls outside the maloca and continues there until the sun rises. At daybreak the dance halts, the girl is released by her protectors, and the feather crown is lifted from her eyes. A shaman presents a firebrand to the girl and instructs her, "Throw it at our enemy." Performance of this gesture is sufficient to break the power of the Noo, and afterward the vorëki can move freely without the protection of others.[51]

The meaning of these gestures and peregrinations appears to depend upon a homology drawn between the local Tukuna environment and their map of the universe. If the seclusion chamber is seen as the underworld, then when the vorëki steps into the maloca she effectively emerges from the subterranean realms to the earth's surface. Here, she stands between the realm of the Noo and that of the sun, still subject more to the former than the latter and still threatened by them. But with another movement—the dance procession outside the maloca—she ascends further, to the realm of the sun. This interpre-

Figure 23. Assault of the Noo. When the initiand is led out from her seclusion chamber, she is confronted by all the masqueraders, dressed as demons, who pursue her in dance steps to the highly rhythmic, aggressive music of stamping tubes, horns and drums. Based on a photograph in Schultz, "Tukuna Maidens Come of Age," p. 631.

tation is supported by three details. First, the ceremony is orchestrated so that the girl will be outside when the sun rises, sunrise being the crucial moment when she (who heretofore was the passive victim of demonic aggression) suddenly counterattacks against her oppressors. Second, at this moment the feather crown, emblem of the sun, which served to shield her eyes from the sun, is lifted, so that she sees and basks in the full glory of the solar realm. Finally, the firebrand that she receives is a solar weapon, containing the sun's fire, and it is with this weapon from the above that she overcomes the demons from below.

A mortal cannot remain in the realm of the sun for long, however, and even Ariana was forced to leave. Her departure is said to have been prompted by her having pulled out two locks of hair from the sun, one blue (or perhaps black) and the other red. A similar fate befalls the vorëki, although in the ritual it is she rather than the sun who has her hair pulled out—perhaps as vengeance for Ariana's audacity.

This occurs rather suddenly at midday, when the sun is highest and strongest. Up to that moment the full company has been dancing outside. The dance is interrupted by the paternal uncle, who grabs a lock of the girl's hair and pulls it out, whereupon all return to the maloca. Once there, the girl is seated at the center of the dwelling upon a tapir skin or bark-cloth mat, where a group of women sit around her and pluck her hair out in little bunches. Painful though this must be, most girls bear it calmly, and the last lock—which is dyed red with urucu dye—is pulled by the uncle. The girl replaces her feather crown above the eyes and the dance begins anew, now madder than ever.[52] The masqueraders, too, take up the dance, but this is their last hurrah. After a short time they remove their costumes and pile them around the vorëki, who is seated once again at the center of the maloca in order to receive this offering. In return the guests are given gifts of smoked meat and fish, which they take eagerly, and reassume their normal demeanor.

Although the main purpose of the rite is the transformation of the vorëki from girl to woman, a transformation takes place in the guests as well, particularly the masqueraders. Having been reduced to the nature of demons—rowdy, violent, obscene—they are restored to their human mode of existence when they discard their costumes. The change is marked by the gift they receive: smoked meat. In innumerable Tukuna tales, demons appear as cannibalistic monsters, eating victims raw or sucking their viscera out through holes bored in their flesh.[53] It is only humans who eat their meat cooked, and, as Lévi-Strauss has shown with such formidable documentation, cooking is perhaps the ultimate mark of civilization.[54] By eating smoked meat—meat that has been cooked so long and so well that it resists decay—the guests become civilized again and reap the benefits of civilization. The dangers of their atavistic reversal are past, and they can once again aid in carrying the initiand toward adulthood.

After the demonic costumes have been abandoned, the community as a whole focuses its protective powers on the vorëki rather than leaving this task to her family alone. All those present who have magic powers of any sort now gesture over the girl for her benefit, as her cosmic journeys are not yet at an end. She is lifted up on the tapir skin and carried to the river nearby. Again, this should be seen in light of the homology between the local terrain and the universe at large. The initiand—who has gone from the underworld (seclusion chamber) to earth (maloca) to sun (outside) and back to earth again, carrying a bit of the sun with her—now embarks for the only realm that remains: the underwater region where dwell the aquatic monsters, Dyëvaë. This realm is represented by the river (Figure 24).

At the river the initiand's mother and her uncle's wife remove all her ornaments and clothing, while shamans stick an arrow in the water four meters offshore in order to defend against the Dyëvaë.[55] The girl kneels naked in the water and is bathed by the shamans. This might be taken as a rite of purification were it not for the fact that the shamans are careful always to pass the water from her feet to her head "to prevent her becoming prematurely pregnant."[56]

The girl then swims about, crawling through the legs of one sha-

Figure 24. The setting for the Moça Nova. The illustration shows the seclusion chamber (A), the corral (B), the maloca (C), the outside area (D) where the initiand first sees the sun after months of seclusion, and the nearby stream or river (E), representing the subaquatic underworld.

man, circling the magic arrow, and diving into deeper water several times. Having mastered the last of the cosmic domains, she returns to the shore, where she is dressed again. The guests demolish the seclusion chamber, sweep up its wreckage with the other debris of the feast, and carry this in armloads to be thrown in the river.

> On this occasion everyone takes a bath without removing his clothes; that is, men, women, and children drag and toss one another into the river. Soon the clayey edge, wetted down by those entering and leaving, becomes so slick that any push is sufficient to force a person to slip into the river. The scene arouses great hilarity and at times has a certain erotic stamp, but it is still an excellent refresher to raise the spirits of those who have drunk to excess.[57]

With this festive scene, the public portion of the ceremony comes to an end. All descend together into the precosmogonic slime, abandon their social distinctions and pretenses, and renounce the serious business of the world; they frolic and emerge refreshed. Shortly thereafter they "change their wet and muddy festive attire for workaday clothing, load their canoes, and leave."[58] For them the ritual is complete, and this is the end of the ceremony as it is currently performed. In the relatively recent past, however, the most important part of the proceedings came after the guests had all departed.

Once the girl was alone with her family she was taken to a fishing spot, where she stood in the water and was bathed again, this time with a solution of the plant commonly called *timbó*, a fish "poison," that changes the surface tension of the water and causes fish to die of suffocation. The myth of Ariana sheds light on this puzzling ritual. Ariana, a young girl who traveled throughout the cosmic realms, provided a model for the initiand's own journeys. As the result of her journey, Ariana succeeded in procuring for the benefit of all mankind a valuable gift: maize. Thus far we have not seen any comparable gift won by the vorëki, and there is no evidence that she repeats Ariana's deed or is associated with maize in any special way.

However, Ariana is not the only heroine of myth whose role is assumed by the Tukuna initiand. Each girl patterns herself, not only on Ariana, but also the young woman who escaped from the Noo in the myth of the origin of masks. There is also a third mythic character who must be considered, particularly in the context of the timbó bath. This is the "Mother of Timbó."

> The relatives of the vorëki took her with them into the jungle in order to pull timbó for her bath. While so occupied they left her sitting on a nodular outgrowth of a timbó root, where she remained waiting the entire time while the relatives were busy in the timbó

stand. Without having had any sexual relations whatsoever she became pregnant by the spirit of the timbó and gave birth to a son. When, after six months, she carried the child for the first time to take a bath in the igarapé [narrow stream or channel], she noticed that as soon as she dipped the little boy into the water, the fish died in great numbers around him. When, in the second bath, this phenomenon was repeated, she realized that the boy was the cause and that he was the son of timbó. From then on she no longer bathed him in the igarapé, for fear that all the fish might die, but bathed him on land. When the boy grew older, his relatives used him to kill fish, allowing him to swim a little in the igarapé.[59]

Each initiand is identified with this woman, who is the prototype of the vorëki about to undergo her timbó bath. Each girl wins the gift of timbó, just as Ariana won the gift of maize. In contrast to Ariana's maize, however, timbó seems to belong to the realm of fishing rather than of agriculture, but its position is a bit more complex because it is itself a plant and thus must also be considered a part of the agricultural world, as well. Its position is further complicated by the fact that the harvesting of plants is exclusively the work of women, whereas fishing is the work of men. Timbó is thus a substance that straddles agriculture and fishing, being a gift from the world of women to that of men.[60]

Although the Tukuna employ other means of fishing—fishhook, javelin, arrow, harpoon—timbó is by far the easiest to use and the most productive. Its efficiency, however, creates the danger of excessive success followed by diminishing returns, for if too many fish are killed not enough will be left to reproduce. Respect for the balance of life dictates moderation in timbó's use, and such moderation is in the Tukuna's best interests in the long run. The Mother of Timbó clearly recognizes this when she sees her son's exceptional powers and renounces any further use of timbó for the killing of fish. As a result, this becomes the proper concern of men (represented in the myth as the woman's relatives, who are undoubtedly understood as being males). They too must show respect for the balance of life and may only use the gift of timbó in moderation; they allow the boy to swim in the igarapé only "a little."

In addition to being a highly efficient fish "poison," timbó has other properties. Most interesting in the present context is the fact that a bath in a timbó solution is believed to render women infertile for a time.[61] It is thus a contraceptive bath that the vorëki takes at the culminating moment of initiation.

Such a practice would be extremely difficult to explain in the rituals of an agricultural people, who value fertility highly. But the world

view of a fishing people such as the Tukuna is quite different from
that of agriculturalists, particularly with regard to the issue of fertility. Rather than being regarded with pure joy, the emergence of reproductive power in a girl evokes mixed emotions. Certainly her new
fertility is valued, because it is requisite for the continuation of
human life and culture, but if unrestrained it poses a serious danger
to the broader totality of life: too many humans will wipe out the
world of nature (fish or game) and will themselves die of sorrow and
starvation soon thereafter.

At once blessing and threat, female fertility is the subject of the
Tukuna Festa das Moças Novas. On the one hand, the initiand is celebrated, made eligible for sexuality and marriage,[62] and encouraged
to produce new life through the example of the new mother in the
myth of the origin of masks, who escaped the wrath of the Noo by
virtue of having just given birth. On the other hand, there are mythic
exemplars who provide the vorëki with quite a different model. No
children are reported for Ariana and no lovers for the virgin Mother
of Timbó. Furthermore, the vorëki is required to be a virgin at the
time of initiation, and within the ceremony conscious steps are taken
to inhibit her future fertility.[63] She is given an upward-flowing bath
by shamans, which reverses the direction of birth, and she concludes
the rite with a contraceptive bath of timbó.

This bath, I believe, is something of a sacrifice in which the initiand
gives up a portion of her fertility for the general welfare of her people
and the universe at large. By renouncing for a time the conception of
children, she benefits the world of nature, permitting the fish population to thrive. But she also makes it possible for people to avail themselves of this increased supply of fish: she becomes the Mother of
Timbó, the most efficient means of fishing.

Timbó and fertility are similar in that they both require moderation; an excess of either threatens the entire balance of life and leads
to disaster for all—people and game alike. These principles are not
immediately evident, and it would be easy for one to overvalue fertility or timbó, reaping their short-term benefits without regard for the
ultimate consequences.

It is only when one possesses a broader, even a cosmic perspective
and appreciates the subtleties of maintaining the balance of life that
one perceives the need for moderation of fertility and timbó. Such a
perspective is the mark of wisdom and maturity, not to be expected in
the young, impetuous, and irresponsible. It is gained only as the result
of broad experience, from contemplation of the universe at large instead of one's personal needs and desires alone.

These reflections provide an understanding of why the vorëki's cosmic journeys are a necessary part of her initiation and why they are only a preparation for her transformation through the timbó bath. It is through her journeys that she gains a truly cosmic perspective, plumbing every realm of the universe in turn. These realms, she learns, are all part of one world, and none can thrive to the exclusion of others. Unmitigated aggression against the inhabitants of other realms is the mark of the demons she meets and overcomes, and, by extension, is a demonic trait in man.

Ideally, such revelations force the initiand to reorganize her view of the world, recognizing and respecting the balance of all living things. Although she is but a small factor in this balance her emergent fertility nevertheless constitutes a threat, and if the balance is to be preserved, moderation will be required of her. In her timbó bath she accepts this need for moderation and wins an invaluable gift in return. The danger of excess averted, her fertility becomes a blessing to all—in the broadest possible sense.

6

The Rape
of
Persephone

Most studies of initiation, or of any ritual, for that matter, are based upon ethnographic evidence: the objective reporting of a living ceremony at first hand. Given a sufficiently skilled and well-trained reporter, this is the most reliable evidence for which one could hope. Such data provided the starting point for analyses of the Navajo, Tiv, and Tukuna initiations in previous chapters, and without the rich, thorough reporting provided by Frisbie, the Bohannons, Nimuendaju, and others, these analyses would have been impossible.

There are, however, certain rituals that were performed in the past but that have fallen into disuse for one reason or another and thus cannot be observed at first hand. This was true of the Tiyyar initiation, last performed in the 1930s and now completely abandoned, yet of great theoretical and historical interest. In order to study the Tiyyar rite it was necessary for Gough to consult older Tiyyar, who had seen the Tālikettukalyāṇam performed, and to reconstruct the ceremony's details on the basis of their testimony. Such an exercise in reconstruction is perfectly legitimate and may be pursued with great confidence if the gap in time that must be bridged is relatively small and can be overcome with the help of informants who were themselves observers or participants.

A much more serious set of problems arises, however, when one wishes to study rituals of the more distant past or of civilizations that have disappeared. In this case the researcher must make use of such evidence as may exist. Some cultures provide us with relatively extensive reports of their rituals in the form of priestly manuals, as do cultures of India and the ancient Near East. Others offer only iconographic evidence, as is the case with the palaeolithic peoples of

71

Europe. Folk dances and customs can also yield valuable information, as they do for the Slavs, Chinese, and ancient peoples of the British Isles. This is not to say that any of these data can provide us with the detailed information that is afforded us by the best ethnographer's reports, but used with caution they permit the whole or partial reconstruction of important rites that would otherwise be lost.[1]

Literary sources, too, may offer valuable testimony. Certain historical, mythological, and narrative texts contain accounts of rituals, occasionally in disguised form but often quite plainly laid out. Modern scholarship has been very successful in reconstructing initiatory scenarios on the strength of such evidence, focusing most often on male initiations but turning increasingly to women's rites.[2]

Roman literature has been particularly productive in this regard, and Greek sources are now being thoroughly reexamined for evidence of women's initiation. Such ceremonies have already been recognized in accounts of the Arrephoria and Brauronia festivals, and in the Thesmophoria and the Haloa—two ceremonies that reenacted details of the Demeter-Persephone mythos.[3]

The well-known myth of Demeter and Persephone is unquestionably the most important myth of classical antiquity to focus on the lives of women, and it is thus possible that it may have been tied to women's rites. At its heart is the bond of two women, mother and daughter, a bond that is ruptured when Persephone is abducted by Hades, lord of the underworld, and reestablished when Demeter's mourning forces the gods to return her daughter. It has been interpreted in many fashions, most often as an allegory of the seasons or of the grain, but most convincingly, in my opinion, by Henri Jeanmaire as the description of a woman's initiation.[4]

This thesis has not gained wide acceptance in classical circles and is today largely ignored.[5] The reason for this, in large measure, is that a view of the Persephone myth as a scenario of women's initiation is not easily reconciled with the well-known fact that in the Mysteries of Eleusis, the most famous ritual associated with the myth, men were initiated as well as women, the Mysteries being open to all who spoke Greek and who had not committed homicide. I must emphasize that it was not Jeanmaire's intent, nor is it mine, to offer an interpretation of the Eleusinian Mysteries, although certain details from the Mysteries are of value to my argument. My chief focus, like Jeanmaire's, is on the myth, for the myth, in our opinion, preserves a state of affairs anterior to that apparent in the Mysteries as historically reported.

It is our contention that a close reading of the texts in which the myth is recounted, especially the *Homeric Hymn to Demeter*, reveals a scenario of a young woman's initiation. Beyond that, it is my hypothesis that at some point in prehistory, probably prior to the arrival of the Indo-Europeans in the Greek regions (ca. 1800 B.C.?), a ritual resembling that described in the myth was actually performed for some or all women in these regions upon their arriving at puberty. Other members of the society, including men, participated in the ritual by taking the roles of other characters in the myth.

Over the course of centuries, however, several major changes in Greek civilization resulted in modifications of this ritual pattern. The first of these was the advent of the Indo-Europeans, whose religious system emphasized male deities, ideologies, and rituals in contrast to the matri-centered religion of the Old European peoples who inhabited Greece before their coming.[6] As a result, rituals that spoke directly to the lives of women must have declined in importance, disappeared entirely, or modified their form. Second, Greece changed from a predominantly tribal society to a predominantly urban one, and this, as Angelo Brelich argued, forced a change in the nature of initiatory rituals, whereby rites of passage that had been mandatory for all youths and that conveyed full membership and adult status in society, became impractical as population increased and as social roles became more differentiated. As a result, these tribal initiations were transformed, becoming elective cults into which individuals might be inducted and through which they would be promised salvation.[7] In other words, puberty initiations became Mystery initiations—precisely the transformation I posit for the rites reflected in the Persephone myth. Third, numerous Greek city-states saw the evolution of democratic institutions and ideals. This was particularly true of Athens, the *polis* to which Eleusis was attached most closely.[8] It is this process of democratization that may have resulted in the opening up of the Eleusinian Mysteries to all save barbarians and murderers.

The Mysteries are thus a totally different type of ritual from those discussed in preceding chapters, but they appear to be the historical descendant of certain rites of women's initiation that are described in the Persephone myth and that resemble the Tiyyar, Navajo, Tiv, and Tukuna examples in many ways. It is the myth, therefore, that is of greatest interest to us.

Jeanmaire's assessment of the myth emerged from an etymological excursus within his monumental work, *Couroi et Courètes*. Having established that Greek *kouros* denoted young boys at the moment of initiation to adult status, he adduced a corresponding meaning for the feminine form of the same word: *kourē* in the Homeric dialect, *korē* in Attic, "young girl of initiatory age." It is this very term that is most often used as a by-name of Persephone.[9] On the basis of this linguistic evidence, Jeanmaire argued that the myth of Persephone's abduction

was nothing other than an account of archaic Greek initiation of
women.

That Persephone is a young girl on the verge of womanhood, and
thus at an appropriate age for initiation, is clear from the texts in
which her myth is related. Her by-name, *korē*, is virtually synonymous
with Greek *parthenos*, "maiden, virgin,"[10] and the Latin sources regularly call her *virgo* or make reference to her *virginitas*.[11] At the same
time, the texts are equally insistent on the fact that the maiden has
reached physical maturity and is thus of marriageable age. The *Homeric Hymn to Demeter*, the oldest, most complete, and most important
version of the Persephone myth, calls the maid *thalerē*, "nubile, rip-
ened" (l. 79) and groups her with the "deep-breasted" (*bathukolpos*)
Okeanids (l. 5). Other sources report that some of the gods had already asked for Persephone's hand,[12] and artistic representations
show a beautiful, full-breasted, teenage girl.

This girl, youthful and innocent, is suddenly and unexpectedly
wrenched away from the world in which she has grown up. One day
while gathering flowers with her playmates—an act that is still a ritual prelude to marriage in the Greek countryside[13]—she is snatched
up and whisked to the underworld, kicking and screaming all the
way. The *Homeric Hymn* begins with this description (ll. 1–23):

I sing of Demeter, she of the lovely hair, a deity worthy of worship,
And the other one, her thin-ankled daughter, whom Aidoneus stole,
    and whom Far-sounding Zeus, whose voice is deep, gave [to him]
Far from Demeter of the golden weapon, she of the splendid fruit,
While she [Kore] was playing with the deep-breasted maidens of
    Okeanos:
Picking blossoms, roses, crocuses, and fair violets
On the gentle meadow, agallis and hyacinth
And narcissus, which Gaia [the earth]—obliging the plans of Zeus for
    Hades—
Sent forth as bait for the blushing maiden.
It was a shining wonder, something awesome to behold
For the immortal gods and for all mortal men.
And from its root, a hundred blooms had grown.
It smelled most sweet and all the wide heavens above
And all the earth and the salt swell of sea rejoiced.
Then, struck with wonder, she reached out both hands
To grasp the fair plaything. And the earth of the wide ways gaped
In the plain of Nysa. Upon her, the lord who greets many [Hades]
    sprang
With his immortal horses, he, the many-named son of Kronos.
He snatched her—she unwilling and lamenting—
In his golden chariot, and she raised her voice in shrill tones,
calling to her father [Zeus], Kronos' son, the highest and most noble.

Not one of the immortals, nor mortal men
Heard her voice, nor the olive trees whose fruit is goodly.[14]

Numerous details should be noted in this passage. The verb used
here, as in all Greek sources, to describe Hades' action is *harpazein* (ll.
3, 19, 56, and elsewhere), meaning "to seize, snatch, carry off," a term
usually reserved for acts of war or thievery, but always acts of violence.[15] In Latin texts, another word connoting violence is found:
raptu, meaning "abduction, seizure, rape."[16]

The assault is thus violent, and the text emphasizes that Kore is
aekousan, "unwilling" (ll. 19, 30, 72). She has been led into a trap. The
beguiling narcissus was the bait, set forth by Gaia according to the
instructions of Zeus (l. 8), and under Hades' powerful attack the
maiden can only cry out, ironically calling to Zeus for assistance
(l. 21).

Kore's companions—her age-mates, the Okeanids—take up this
cry, according to the *Homeric Hymn* (l. 27), and the earliest known artistic representation of the myth, a painted wine cup from Phaistos
dating from the middle Minoan period (just before 2000 B.C.), shows
two companions crying out while Kore disappears into the earth's
chasm beside the "flower of deception" (Figure 25).[17] Other sources,
however, place the goddesses Athene and Artemis beside Persephone
and tell how these deities try to oppose Hades and protect their com-
panion because, according to Claudian (*De Raptu Proserpine* 2.207f),
"Their common virginity goads them to arms and makes them bitter

Figure 25. The earliest known depiction of the Persephone myth, a
middle Minoan cup from Phaistos, ca. 2000 B.C. Kore's companions,
most probably the goddesses Artemis and Athene, are shown in pos-
tures of alarm as she disappears into a vagina-shaped chasm in the
earth. In the lower right is a fantastic, highly sexualized flower, sent
up by the earth in order to lure Kore into the trap. Adapted from
Caroly Kerenyi, *Eleusis* (copyright 1967), p. xix. Reprinted by permission of Princeton University Press.

at the crime of the wild ravisher."[18] Their heroic defense is stopped, however, by Zeus with a blast of thunder.[19]

Deceived by her father, abandoned by her companions, Kore looks to her mother for help. As soon as Demeter learns of her daughter's fate she runs to give aid, but by then it is too late and the girl has disappeared below the earth's surface. Demeter laments, grieving for Kore as if she were dead but searching for her nonetheless. The description in the *Homeric Hymn* (ll. 38–50) is particularly moving:

The tops of the mountains and the depths of the sea echoed
Under her [Kore's] immortal voice, and her mother, the Lady, heard.
And now sharp sorrow seized her heart, and she rent
The headdress round her ambrosial hair with her own hands,
And she threw a dark veil over both her shoulders.
She rushed like a bird over the broad earth and the sea,
Searching. And no one was willing to tell her the truth,
Neither from the gods nor mortal men,
Nor birds—did any true messenger come to her.
For nine days thereafter, Lady Deo [Demeter] roamed about the
    earth.
She kindled torches in her hands
And never did she partake of ambrosia and sweet-tasting nectar
While grieving, nor did she lustrate her body.

This heart-rending concern of Kore's mother stands in marked contrast to the attitude of the girl's father, Zeus, who planned the abduction himself and approved of it from the outset. This contrast in parental attitudes is already evident in the earliest version of the myth, Hesiod's three-line account (*Theogony*, ll. 912–914):

Then he [Zeus] came to the bed of Demeter, she who feeds many,
And she gave birth to white-armed Persephone, whom Aidoneus
Snatched away from beside her mother, and Zeus the counselor
    granted it.[20]

This set of circumstances, in which a father instigates the abduction of his daughter, against the wishes of the girl and her mother, has always posed a difficult problem for interpretation. Some scholars have been inclined to see a hidden enmity between the celestial father god Zeus and the terrestrial mother goddess Demeter, perhaps dating back to the opposition of Indo-European and pre-Indo-European, or of Olympian and Chthonic religious forms.[21] Such a formulation, however, merely provides a possible historical background for what is a very live and important issue in the myth: Zeus and Demeter disagree violently as to what shall be the proper fate of their daughter. Although most texts seem to follow the *Homeric Hymn* and sympathize with Demeter, there is no reason to view Zeus's actions as sinister or perverse. He is Kore's parent no less than Demeter, and since he is consistently pictured as a loving parent—witness the tears of blood he sheds at the death of his son, Sarpedon (*Iliad* 16.458–461)—it is fully possible that he has the girl's best interests at heart no less than her mother.

Zeus's view of what is good for Kore is quite different from that of Demeter, however, and to understand this we must confront a basic fact of Greek kinship ideology. The Greeks believed that there was a profound difference between mother and father, the former being seen as the biological parent, who gave birth, and the latter as the social parent, who gave and continues to give his children a place in the world throughout their lives.[22] As part of this role, the Greek father arranged marriages, transferring daughters from his own household to that of another man, and from the status of daughter to that of wife.

On the strength of this, some scholars have interpreted the Persephone myth as the description of a marriage, but this is unlikely in view of the other family connections stated in the myth.[23] Hades, Zeus, and Demeter are siblings, children of Kronos and Rheia (*Theogony*, 453–458; *Hymn to Demeter*, ll. 85, 364). Persephone's abductor is thus both her maternal and paternal uncle (*mētrōs* and *patrōs*), and as such an unlikely mate; an uncle's chief role was to care for his niece or nephew in a protective way.[24] To be sure, Demeter does not view Hades' action as protective or helpful, but from the standpoint of Zeus, Hades acts properly, undertaking the dangerous task of transforming Kore from child to woman. In this, he is like the father's brother among the Tukuna, who also presides over his niece's initiation.

When first we see Kore after her abduction she is in the underworld. In contrast to the detailed description of her capture the sources offer little on what her existence is like in the subterranean realms, regularly referred to as "the murky gloom," *zophos ēeroeis* (ll. 80, 337, 402, 464). Those who favored a view of her myth as seasonal allegory interpreted her stay in the underworld as a mythopoeic description of winter, the time when the crops are underground. This view has fallen into disfavor, since Kore disappears while gathering flowers—thus in spring or early summer—and her absence cannot correspond to wintertime.[25]

Another interpretation is possible, however. As we have seen in our study of the Tukuna, an initiand's time and place of seclusion may be referred to as "being in the underworld."[26] Such terminology is probably used for a number of reasons. Often, the initiand is believed to experience literal or figurative death and rebirth through initiation. In other scenarios, a live initiand is expected to visit all or many of the cosmic realms, the underworld always being included in the tour. The underworld is thought to be a less well-defined place than the land of the living—"hazy" or "murky," and thus well-suited to a person whose place in society is equally ill-defined. The initiand is a person in limbo, who has lost one status but not yet received another to take its place.[27] Having lost her home, her parents, her playmates, indeed all the world she knew, Kore is in just such a position.

Kore suffers another loss in the "underworld," a loss that dramatically alters her status and even her name: the loss of her virginity. Claudian is perhaps clearest on this point; according to him, as she is carried underground, the maiden laments (*De Raptu Proserpine* 2.260–264):

O fortunate are those girls whom other ravishers
Have borne off! At least they have delight in the usual daylight.
But along with my virginity, the sky is taken from me;
My purity is snatched away with the light, and I must depart from
    earth
As I am led captive into slavery for the Stygian tyrant.

The *Homeric Hymn* is a bit more coy on this point, but no less clear. When first we see Persephone after her abduction (ll. 343–344), she is in a compromising position:

> [Hades] was sitting in bed with his venerable bedmate,
> Much against her will, and yearning for her mother.

A terser or more poignant description of a young girl betwixt and between could not be imagined: unhappy with her bedmate, he being her *parakoitis* as well as she his, yearning for her mother, yet unable ever to return to her former mode of being.[28] Kore's defloration changes her utterly. She has, in effect, been initiated by rape, a pattern found in a number of male-centered, misogynistically inclined cultures, and strongly suggested in numerous Greek myths.[29] Introduction to productive sexuality seems to be only a secondary motive for such practices, the real point being the forcible subjugation of women to male control, as has been brilliantly argued by J. S. La Fontaine with reference to women's initiation among the Gisu of East Africa:

> Defloration causes a flow of blood and is an essential prerequisite to conception, as Gisu recognize. It is thus an event of the same physical order as menstruation and childbirth; it is evidence of the dangerous and creative power of women. Yet it differs from other similar ritualized events in one very important particular. The

defloration of a woman is not, in the same sense that menstruation and childbirth are natural events, a natural event. It involves a deliberate human act to induce it. It is thus the point at which control by the society of the physical power of women is greatest, for the timing and circumstances can be socially determined in a way that the other physical events in a woman's life cannot be. In a male-dominated society such as that of the Gisu this is vitally important and is, I suggest, the reason why defloration, rather than other events, is made the focus of the most important *rite de passage* for women.[30]

Ancient Greece was no less male-dominated than is Gisu society, and Hades is no tender bridegroom who lovingly takes his bride to bed but rather is the male oppressor who forces his will upon a young girl for the first time, thus teaching her proper submission to all members of his sex.

Her virginity lost, Kore's name, which literally means "the maiden," becomes highly inappropriate, and she takes on a new name: Persephone. This dual name for one goddess has long given scholars pause, some arguing that one is her name as Hades' wife, the other as Demeter's daughter;[31] others that two historically separate deities, one Indo-European and one pre-Indo-European, must have merged.[32] But if one is willing to exclude the two passages of the *Homeric Hymn to Demeter* in which the goddess Hekate appears (and this has been urged for more than eighty years on the basis of strong textual, linguistic, and religious-historical grounds) then the problem is easily resolved.[33] For once this is done, the text never refers to Demeter's daughter as "Persephone" until the moment at which Hermes is sent as a messenger from Zeus to bring her back to earth (l. 337)—which is to say, the moment when the end of her initiation draws near. Thereafter, she always bears this new name, with only one exception: Zeus calls her "Kore" when referring to the time each year she will have to spend with Hades in the underworld (l. 445)—that is, when she will reassume her role as initiand (or perhaps, better yet, when a new initiand will assume the role of Kore).

It thus appears that prior to her stay with Hades Persephone has no proper name, being known only by her status: *korē*, "the maiden, the virgin, the young girl." The girl's proper name is bestowed on her only after she has been initiated, become an adult, lost her maiden status. Such a change of name is a regular feature in the initiatory rites of innumerable peoples as a mark of the initiand's total transformation.[34]

If we are told little about Persephone while she is in the nether regions, the same is not true with regard to Demeter during this same span of time. According to the *Homeric Hymn*, the goddess dons a dark headdress in mourning, takes torches, and searches all the world, never pausing to eat or drink. She breaks her fast only when her search brings her to Eleusis, where a servant girl's jests cause her to laugh for the first time since she has lost her daughter. The *Homeric Hymn* tells the story with some reserve, as befits its lofty style (ll. 200–211):

She [Demeter] was unlaughing, and did not partake of food or drink,
As she was wasting away with yearning for her deep-girt daughter,
Until noble Iambe, joking with many jests,
Made the holy lady
Smile then, and have a joyous spirit,
And she [Iambe] ws pleasing in spirit to her thereafter.
And Metaneira gave her a cup filled with
Honey-sweet wine, but she refused it, for she said it was not fitting
For her to drink the red wine, and she bade them give her water
And barley mixed with fresh penny-royal for her to drink.
And she [Metaneira] prepared this kykeon for the goddess, as she
   [Demeter] had requested.
And Deo, the lady of many, accepted it for the sake of the rite.

A more explicit version of this incident is given by Clement of Alexandria, who quotes a verse attributed to Orpheus which describes the same scene. In Clement's account, however, (*Protreptikos* 2.17–18), the raucous Baubo—whose name literally means "vagina" or "a mock vagina, counterpart to a dildo (*baubōn*)," and who is represented in art with dramatic emphasis on her genitals (Figure 26)—replaces the more sedate Iambe, whose name is derived from the iambic meters used in all Greek jesting verse.[35] Of Baubo, Clement reports: "Speaking thus, she hoisted up her robes and displayed all of her body, a shape that was not fitting. And the child Iakkhos was there and he was laughing as he kept thrusting his hand under Baubo's breasts. And truly, when the goddess [Demeter] saw this, she smiled in her spirit, and she took up the shining vessel in which the *kykeon* was contained."[36]

Such a scene was naturally considered scandalous by the good church father, who reported it only to show the obscenity of the pagan Mysteries. It is likely that by the time Clement wrote (second century A.D.), most pagans themselves no longer understood the significance of this ritual gesture. But as is well known, such "obscene" gestures are often found in connection with women's initiation and women's secret societies, enacted by women who are otherwise the soul of propriety.[37]

What seems to be expressed in this fashion is the understanding that when a young woman comes of age, or when women come together in the absence of men, the force of their sexuality is so great

Figure 26. Terracotta figure of Baubo from Priene, fifth century B.C. True to the etymology of her name ("vagina, mock vagina"), Baubo is always represented as the personification of the female genitals. Yet although her femininity is put at the center of the figurine while all other details save a haunting smile are stripped away, the piece evokes ideas of androgyny through its markedly phallic shape, reminiscent of Baubo's implied male counterpart, Baubon ("dildo"). Based on a photograph in Neumann, *The Great Mother* (copyright 1955), plate 48. Reprinted by permission of Princeton University Press.

that it can no longer be suppressed. Although social norms may severely inhibit the direct expression of female sexual energy under ordinary circumstances, at these special moments it bursts forth in "obscene" gestures, songs, and stories, whereby women collectively celebrate the appearance of reproductive power in a new woman. Thus, when Demeter mourns the loss of her daughter, she simultaneously celebrates her transformation.

Once cheered, Demeter agrees to remain at the court of Keleos and Metaneira in Eleusis, tending their son, Demophon. Her care is more than that of an ordinary nurse, however: by day she anoints the prince with ambrosia to make him immortal, and by night she lays him in the fire to burn away his mortality. In the latter act, however, she is interrupted by Metaneira, who cries out, thinking that the stranger is harming her child. Startled, Demeter reveals herself in her divine form and then allows Demophon to die.

This episode is something of an excursus to the Persephone myth in which it is set, but it is not a near-pointless rambling, as some have claimed.[38] Rather, it is intended as a deliberate counterpoint to the Persephone story, being itself the account of an initiation that in many ways is diametrically opposed to that of Persephone. Whereas hers is the initiation of an adolescent, Demophon's is that of an infant; hers is of a woman, his is of a boy; hers aims at attaining maturity, his at immortality; hers is planned and executed by close relatives, his by a stranger; and finally, hers is successful, while his is not. The two initiations stand in the starkest contrast to one another, and between them they define what initiation should and should not be.[39]

The failed initiation of Demophon has other important effects, as Demeter's anger at Metaneira for interfering leads her to demand that a temple be built, the temple that will later house the Mysteries of Eleusis, the most famous and important rituals of the ancient world (ll. 270–274). The temple is not enough to placate her for the loss of Kore, however, as the *Homeric Hymn* makes clear (ll. 302–313):

But golden Demeter
Was sitting there [in her temple], far from all the blessed gods
And she remained there, wasting away with longing for her deep-girt
  daughter.
She produced for men a most grim year upon the fruitful earth,
And a year most dog-like, and the earth could send up no seed at all,
For fair-crowned Demeter hid [the seed] away.
Many cattle pulled the curved ploughs in vain over the fields,
And much bright barley fruitlessly entered the earth,
And she would have destroyed the race of men completely
With painful hunger, and would have robbed those who dwell on
  Olympos
Of the glorious recompense of gifts that give honor, and of sacrifices,
Had not Zeus perceived this and noted it in his spirit.

If it had not already been such, the rape of Persephone now becomes a truly cosmic event. The famine plunges the world into a state of chaos, and threatens the existence of men and gods alike.[40] The crops disappear; the seasons turn topsy-turvy; the earth swallows, but does not bring forth. All life hangs in the balance, and even Zeus cannot stand up under such pressure.

At first, Zeus dispatches messengers who attempt to dissuade Demeter from her anger, but when this proves impossible he decides to yield. He sends Hermes, guide of souls, to Hades, telling him to give up the girl, whom Hermes leads back to earth. Persephone's father—who instigated her initiation—thus calls it to a halt and restores her to the society that she left. This restoration is accomplished gradually, Persephone first coming to earth and rejoining Demeter, with whom she spends an entire day

Comforting one another very much in heart and spirit,
Showing love to one another. And thus she [Demeter] relinquished
  her sorrowing spirit.
They gave and received joy beside each other.

Artistic representations show Persephone emerging from the earth, like a child being born or like the crops coming up (Figure 27), an expression of the facts that Persephone is, in effect, reborn, and that her return causes—and ultimately is synonymous with—the return of the crops after Demeter's famine and, by extension, their return each year in the spring. Her return and the return of vegetative life thus put an end to the state of chaos that her disappearance inaugurated.

The great majority of sources make a point much stronger than that of the *Homeric Hymn,* maintaining that it is at this moment that Demeter first teaches mortals the secrets of agriculture. Previously they lived on what they could gather—roots, berries, acorns, and the like—but now, at Eleusis, they are taught the use of seed and plow by the goddess herself.[41] This knowledge she entrusts to Triptolemos, one of the Eleusinian leaders, charging him to carry it to all peoples of the world, a scene frequently portrayed in sculpture and painting (Figure 28).

Figure 27. Persephone's return, as depicted on an Attic red figured vase dating from about 440 B.C. Hermes, guide of souls (second from left), leads Persephone (far left) from the underworld through a vagina-shaped fissure, signifying her rebirth. Hekate (second from right) then leads the girl by torchlight to her waiting mother (far right). This picture differs from the account of the *Homeric Hymn to Demeter* in three important regards, as noted by Richter, and may thus represent a separate version of the mythic tradition: (1) Demeter waits calmly instead of rushing to meet her daughter; (2) Persephone and Hermes arrive on foot, not in a chariot; (3) Hekate takes an active part in the return, rather than merely appearing afterwards. From a drawing in Richter, *Red-Figured Athenian Vases,* plate 124.

Figure 28. The mission of Triptolemos. Demeter (left), bestows the first grain upon Triptolemos, one of the chief Eleusinian leaders, in celebration of the return of Persephone, who stands at right holding torches. Here, Triptolemos holds a plow, reemphasizing his role as the original recipient of agricultural knowledge. In other vase paintings he is shown with the winged chariot in which he carried this knowledge to all humanity. From a drawing in Harrison, *Prolegomena to the Study of Greek Religion*, p. 273.

This transition from gathering to agriculture is, of course, a shift from chaos to cosmos, nature to culture, or savagery to civilization.[42] As such, it corresponds to Persephone's move from the underworld to earth, and finally to Olympos, as well as her transformation from maiden to adult. It further corresponds to another gift bestowed on humanity by Demeter upon her daughter's return, a gift that the *Homeric Hymn* chooses to emphasize at the expense of her gift of agriculture: the establishment of the Mysteries of Eleusis (ll. 471–482).

Straightway she [Demeter] sent up fruit from the fertile fields,
And all the broad earth was heavy with leaves
And with flowers. And making her way to the lawmaking kings,
She revealed to Triptolemos and Diokles, smiter of horses,
And mighty Eumolpus and Keleos, commander of the host,
The performance of the sacred things and showed them all the rites.
These are respected, and one is not to transgress or profane them
Or divulge them in any way, since a great respect for the gods restrains speech.
Fortunate is he among earthly men who has gazed upon these things,
And he who has not accomplished the sacred things, who has no share in them,
He does not possess a like portion once he is dead beneath the hazy gloom.

This accomplished, the initiation is complete. Persephone has been transformed, humanity has been transformed, the cosmos has been remade. Only then can the final restoration take place (ll. 483–486):

And when all this was communicated, the goddesses
Left to go to Olympos, to the assembled company of the other gods,
And there they dwell beside Zeus, hurler of the thunderbolt,
Respected and worthy of reverence.

Persephone is thus restored to her mother, her father—toward whom there is no trace of bitterness—her home, and all she left; but she is no longer the same maiden who was taken from them. She will never be Kore, the maiden, again. She has matured, become sexualized, died, and been reborn. The myth expresses this transformation in a striking image.

Although ordered to release Persephone and having no choice but to obey Zeus's command, Hades is loath to give up his prize. He conspires to tie Persephone to him by a stratagem that will force her to return for a portion of each year. To this end, he gives her something to eat—a pomegranate seed—and for reasons that are unclear, she is obligated as a result to spend one-third of each year in the underworld.[43]

Why should a tiny seed have such profound effects? The pomegranate seed, like the Navajo corn cake, is a highly complex image that reconciles all manner of opposites into a transcending totality. Bright red, the pomegranate is an image of bloody death in numerous Greek myths and rites, as Kerenyi has shown.[44] Here, however, it is the seed that is specified rather than the fruit as a whole, and any seed, being germinative and productive, inevitably gives rise to ideas of life and rebirth. Furthermore, the red color evokes associations not only of mortal wounds but also of menstrual blood, the blood of defloration, and the blood of parturition: blood of life as well as of death, sexual blood, women's blood. The prodigious number of seeds within a pomegranate has always made it a symbol of exuberant female fertility,[45] but there are male associations as well, for the term used in the *Homeric Hymn* to mean "seed," *kokkos* (ll. 372, 412), can also mean "testicle"—the male organ that produces abundant seed and that is no less vital to fertility than its female counterpart.[46]

Death, life, male, female, and, above all, the irrepressible power of reproduction—are all found in the image of the pomegranate seed. It is this seed that Persephone takes within her body, literally incorporating it into her own being. With this seed, she becomes a new person: whole, mature, fertile, and infinitely more complex than before. Having tasted it, she has crossed a barrier from which there can be no turning back, and nothing Demeter can do will ever make her the same again.

The famed Mysteries of Eleusis present additional evidence for interpreting the Persephone myth as a scenario of women's initiation.

These rites, in large part, have never ceased to be mysteries. Initiates were forbidden to speak of what they had seen and done during the celebration of these rites, and, as Mylonas observed, "the ancient world has kept its secret well."[47] Still, from bits and pieces of evidence that have survived—artistic representations, architectural designs, and scattered literary testimonies—it is possible to get some idea of what transpired at the Greater Mysteries held in Eleusis.[48]

After preliminary purifications, the Mystai, dressed in black in the earliest periods, traveled in procession from Athens to Eleusis along the route traveled by Demeter, finishing their journey by torchlight.[49] Before reaching the temple precinct, they had to cross a bridge, where the procession—preceded by a statue of Iakkhos—was met by people who had their heads covered and who hurled obscene jests and insults at the most important citizens present, much to the delight of the other participants.[50] This moment of levity and mirth is clearly a repetition of the joking in the Baubo/Iambe incident, as well as an intriguing moment of social inversion, and thus of chaos or *akosmia*. For nine days the Mystai fasted, again repeating the actions of Demeter, ending their fast, as did she, with the drinking of the *kykeon*. According to Clement of Alexandria (*Protreptikos* 2.18), before entry to the final rites, each participant had to pronounce a password (*synthema*): "I fasted, I drank the *kykeon*."[51] In all this, most of the Mystai take the role of Demeter, in effect becoming the goddess in her search for her daughter, while certain of their number assume the identity of other figures in the myth. The jesters at the bridge become Baubo; the participants in dances become the young daughters of Keleos and Metaneira who led Demeter to Eleusis;[52] a young boy chosen by lot helped lead the procession, and, given his title of *pais aph' hestias*, "boy of the hearth," one must assume he has become Demophon;[53] and the priests of Eleusis became the first rulers of the city, those to whom Demeter first entrusted the rites.[54] All the participants stepped outside their own historical time and reentered the time of the myth, shedding their individual identities to "partake of the experience of the Goddesses."[55] The situation was quite like that of the Navajo Kinaaldá, where the participants again become the Holy People at Emergence Rim.

If the Mystai in large measure repeated the experiences of Demeter, she must, as Kerenyi put it, be understood as the first Eleusinian initiate: "Her initiation was the finding of her daughter."[56] But is there any evidence that this experience was also repeated in the course of the Mysteries?

All the sources are in agreement that the culmination of the Mysteries was a revelation in which something was displayed to the assembled crowd. The high priest of Eleusis was, in fact, known as the *hierophant,* "he who makes the sacred things appear,"[57] and the plan of the Anaktoron and Telesterion at Eleusis, where the final rites took place, is ingeniously designed for the production of such a spectacle (Figure 29).[58] There is, however, some disagreement as to just what was displayed in this revelation. Tertullian states that it was a phallus, Hippolytos that it was a grain of wheat.[59] Either one of these would be in keeping with the general symbolism and ideology of the Mysteries and the Persephone myth. But the logic of the ceremony seems to require something in addition to these icons, for if the Mystai effectively became Demeter in her search, and if the ceremony ended in joy and celebration, then it is only the recovery of the lost Persephone that could produce such a result.

Such a conclusion is fully supported by an important papyrus of the second century A.D., which recounts a legend already hinted at in Euripides' *Herakles,* line 613. According to Euripides, Herakles was refused admission to the Eleusinian Mysteries, and in the papyrus Herakles tells why he has no need of these ceremonies. The text is as follows:

> [These are] the words of Herakles when he was not
> Allowed to be initiated into the Eleusinian Mysteries:
> "I was initiated a long time ago." Shut out from
> The Eleusinian rites, he carries a torch and resents
> The sacred night. "I was initiated
> To truer Mysteries than the multitude
> ... excellent. And the
> ... beside me, the night to me
> ... And I [will tell] you many
> [Things] I saw. I saw of that
> ... nearby through the night,
> [I saw] the fire, whence
> ... [and] I saw Kore."[60]

Despite the lacunae in the text, it is possible to make out what Herakles is saying. He claims that he has no need of initiation into the Mysteries, for he has already seen what they have to offer, having beheld Kore when he descended into the underworld on the twelfth of his labors.[61] A scholium of Apollodoros of Athens on Theokritos suggests the same conclusion, stating that the final revelation at Eleusis was the appearance of Persephone herself, who was called forth by striking a huge gong.[62]

Such a gong was used in Athenian theater to simulate the crash of thunder, and in the Eleusinian context, Otto argues, it signified the bursting open of the underworld.[63] The fire that Herakles refers to in

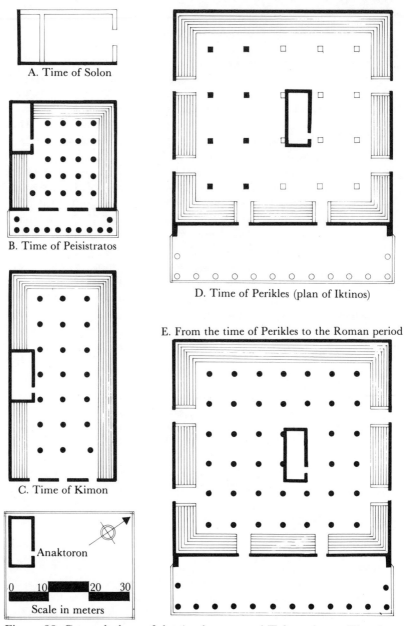

A. Time of Solon

B. Time of Peisistratos

C. Time of Kimon

D. Time of Perikles (plan of Iktinos)

E. From the time of Perikles to the Roman period

Anaktoron

0   10   20   30
Scale in meters

Figure 29. Ground plans of the Anaktoron and Telesterion at Eleusis, where the final revelations of the Mysteries took place. Although there was considerable expansion of the building from the time of Solon (elected Arkhon 595 B.C.) to that of Perikles (ruled 461–429 B.C.), the basic pattern remained unchanged. The Mystai would congregate in the larger Telesterion, but were refused entry into the inner sanctum of the Anaktoron, which was reserved for the hierophant. The inside of the Anaktoron was partially visible through a small door, at which a woman representing or incarnating the returned Persephone presumably appeared. Adapted from Kerenyi, *Eleusis* (copyright 1967), p. 86. Reprinted by permission of Princeton University Press.

the text above, seems to have been dramatic stage lighting for the goddess' epiphany. This spectacle must have excited awe and reverence in the Mystai, who, having become Demeter, mourned as she mourned, searched as she searched, suddenly received their daughter back in a blaze of light.

But who played the part of Persephone in this drama? It is unlikely that a statue represented the goddess, for no such statue has ever been found at Eleusis. It thus becomes highly probable, if not demonstrable with absolute certainty, that a young woman of appropriate age took the role of Persephone, or better yet, *became* Persephone within the Mysteries. Perhaps a priestess or the daughter of a noble Athenian family performed this service—there is no way to be sure.

If such a woman took on the part of Persephone, however, she must have symbolically repeated the experiences of Persephone, just as the Mystai repeated the experiences of Demeter and just as each Navajo girl repeats those of Changing Woman. She went through the same initiation as had the goddess, and each time the Mysteries were enacted the world was transformed along with her—the crops were renewed, the seasons were reestablished, sexuality and fertility recommenced, and all those who were present were beatified by the event.[64]

At an earlier period in history, before the evolution of the Greek city-state, it is possible that every woman took on the role of Persephone, experiencing her initiatory ordeal in symbolic or even literal form. Certainly the goddess' myth and cult can be traced further back than the Eleusinian Mysteries, even though there is evidence of the latter as early as 1500 B.C.[65] The great increase in population that came with *polis*-organization and colonial expansion might then have resulted in a narrowing of an originally broader set of initiatory practices: henceforth one maiden each year took on the part of the goddess, as a symbol and representative of all Eleusinian, Athenian, or Greek maidens. To be sure, such a theory is no more than conjecture, but a similar development has been convincingly demonstrated in the case of other Greek rites of women's initiation, the Brauronia and Arrephoria festivals.[66]

Unlike the other case studies we have examined, the Mysteries do not enable one to formulate a detailed description of the ways in which initiation transformed the initiand. My reconstruction is highly conjectural, even on so basic a point as whether Greek women ever actually went through such rites. The myth of Persephone, however, offers safer ground. If ever it be shown—through archaeological discoveries at Eleusis or elsewhere, or perhaps through the long-awaited decipherement of Linear A—that Greek maidens did take the part of the goddess in an initiatory drama, then the interpretation presented here could be extended to such initiands.

For her part, the mythic Persephone undergoes the same dramatic transformation that we noted in the Tiyyar, Navajo, Tiv, and Tukuna ceremonies. As a result of her initiation, she changes status—from girl to woman, and in the process her very being is transformed as she becomes fertile, productive, experienced, and whole.

Moreover, it is not just this one initiand who is transformed; the entire world is remade as a result of her initiation. Threats of chaos and desolation are warded off, the gifts of civilization come into being, the fruits of the earth spring forth with renewed abundance, and the rhythm of the seasons is established. Persephone's initiation, like that of Changing Woman or the Mother of Timbó (and like that of every Navajo or Tukuna woman who assumes th e roles in the course of her initiation), is perceived as a cosmic event. If ever a Greek woman became Persephone in the same sense that the Mystai at Eleusis became Demeter, it was no trivial, purely personal matter, but something that was felt to affect all the universe.

On the
Nature of
Women's
Initiations

Five examples are hardly sufficient for the formulation of sweeping generalizations, and certain types of conclusion clearly lie beyond the scope and intention of this study. I am thinking particularly of statistical correlations between the existence or nonexistence of women's initiation with different features of society. It has been argued, for instance, that such rituals are more likely to be found among matrilocal peoples than among those who are patrilocal, and while my data have little to offer to support this view, intuitively I am inclined to believe that such is the case.[1] Similarly, I suspect that initiation of women is more likely to be practiced by agriculturalists than by those who derive their subsistence in other ways, but I can hardly demonstrate that this is so. Hunters, fishers, pastorialists, and others also perform women's initiations, often in quite spectacular ways.[2]

My general sense is that the presence of women's initiation in a given culture is a mark of the importance of women within that culture and of the culture's willingness to recognize this publicly and institutionally. Such is certainly true with regard to the Tiyyar, Navajo, Tiv, and Tukuna, although the position of Greek women was considerably less favorable.[3] But five cases are not nearly adequate for conclusions of this sort: one might just as well say that those peoples whose name begins with the letter *T* are inclined to practice women's initiation, since sixty percent of my examples obey this "rule."

Other types of conclusions can more justifiably be drawn on the basis of a limited sample—conclusions that are more qualitative than quantitative, that search more for understanding and appreciation than for correlations having predictive value. For conclusions of such nature, a few examples, carefully chosen and pursued in detail, are of infinitely greater worth than a horde of examples summarily assessed in checklist fashion. For my purposes, depth of understanding is of considerably greater value than breadth of data. I wish to offer three types of conclusions: typological, morphological, and teleological— which is to say, assessments of the varieties of female initiatory rituals, their underlying structure or pattern, and their ultimate purpose.

It may be noted that these three categories of conclusion correspond roughly to three of the fundamental "causes" or "explanatory factors" (*aitia*) posited by Aristotle for all existent matter: morphology, the study of form (*eidos* or *paradeigma*); typology, the study of material or content (*hylē*); and teleology, the end or purpose (*telos*) of a given thing.[4] Aristotle also posits a fourth "cause" of all things: an agent (*hothen*—"whence, from whom or what") who creates a given phenomenon or sets an act in motion. This category of agent is worth considering before we move to the other three areas.

The question of the agent is a fairly straightforward one: Who is it that initiates young women when they come of age?[5] This simple query conceals a host of serious implications. For if men initiate women, then female initiation must be seen as an act imposed on women from outside, an indoctrination, a subjugation, an assault. If it is men who are the effective agents, then initiands must be understood as the victims of their initiators, passive objects who are remade according to the tastes and desires of people quite different from themselves.[6] Under such circumstances initiation becomes a rite of oppression.

Conversely, if women initiate women, the situation is quite different. For if women act independently as agent (excluding a situation in which they act only as surrogates for men), then women's initiation must be seen as something celebrated collectively rather than imposed from outside. It becomes a rite of solidarity, in which women set themselves apart from men, affirming themselves and their differentness from the males around them. Rather than an act of oppression, initiation becomes an act of unity, of resistance, of commiseration.

Practice, however, is not so clear-cut as these hypothetical alternatives suggest. In the rites we have examined, as in the vast majority of others of which I am aware, it is not a case of *either* men *or* women being in charge of the ceremony, but of both sexes having responsibility for specific parts of the rite. Thus, for instance, among the Tiv, it is a man who cuts the scars on the initiand, but it is the girl's mother who takes her to the man who will do this. Again, among the Navajo, whereas a man usually presides at the all-night sing,[7] women are responsible for molding the girl, dressing her, and preparing the circular corn cake, and are present along with men at every step of the ritual. The situation among the Tiyyar and Tukuna is similar, while priests and priestesses alike served in the Eleusinian Mysteries, just as men and women were both admitted as Mystai.

It is not just one sex or the other that acts as agent, nor is it any single individual. Rather, it is the totality of the social order, although the precise nature of the actions taken may be determined by the individual actor's sex. All the rites we have examined are open to men and women, and both sexes take active parts in all of them. It is society as a whole that acts, and thus the initiand experiences both the repressive force of men (who may cut her, rape her, or simply force her to run, work, or stay up all night) and the support of her fellow women (who may dress and adorn her, bring food to her, or keep vigil with her).

In Tukuna initiations, for example, men impersonate demonic beings and assault the initiand, or terrify her with the secret horns said to be demons' voices, while women play quite a different part. The night before the initiand is to emerge from seclusion, a group of women enter her chamber, dress her, and parade around her as she kneels, tapping her gently with leaves in token of their solidarity with her, and shouting joyously upon conclusion of this circumambulation.[8] Later, most of the girl's hair is pulled out by a group of women seated around her, but the first and last locks are taken by her father's brother, who stands above her.[9] The women are thus identified with the initiand: they sit as she sits, forming a group, and all of them have suffered what she now suffers. In contrast, the man is the instigator of the ordeal, and the only one who can put it to an end. He is set above the initiand, physically as well as hierarchically. What he does, he does as an individual rather than as part of a group, and never will he experience the pain he inflicts.

Such distinctions, antagonisms, and tensions are always present in women's initiation, where the initiand becomes to a certain extent the field on which the battle of the sexes is enacted. These tensions exist in all societies, as do many similar tensions: young and old, rich and poor, those of high status and those of low. All of these find expression within the performance of various rituals. Such tensions, however, are never resolved in rituals, nor are conflicts pushed to conclusion. Rather, as Max Gluckman has phrased it, ritual serves "to cloak the fundamental conflicts," to create the appearance that they never existed in the first place, permitting society to maintain its sense of solidarity.[10] Thus, although the conflicting claims of men and women to the soul of the initiand are evident at numerous points, participants on the whole act as members of the broader society, rather than as members of one specific sex. Society as a whole is the agent in women's initiation, acting to preserve the stability of the social collectivity rather than pursuing the specific interests of either gender.

What types of action does society take? In what forms does women's initiation commonly appear? On the strength of the examples presented above, I suggest four basic types. To be sure, these are not exclusive categories, rigidly separated one from another, nor is the list exhaustive, for other types may well exist. Most rites partake of two or more of these four types, combining them in new and creative ways, resulting in endless variety. As I see them, the basic types are bodily mutation, identification with a mythic heroine, cosmic journey, and play of opposites.

Simplest of these is bodily mutation, in which the initiand's body is taken as the locus of her very being, and the transformation desired for her is effected on her physical self. Such action is, of course, suggested by the events of puberty, whereby the body transforms itself, and bodily mutation does seem to be practiced primarily by those among whom the performance of women's initiation is signaled by menarche.

The body is thus treated as something essential, inseparable from the inner self, rather than something foreign, inconsequential, or hostile to the spirit. Moreover, the body is taken as something dynamic, capable of dramatic and—what is more important—meaningful change. Such changes may be produced by nature (menarche, the development of breasts, widening of hips, or appearance of pubic hair), but they may also be produced by human action. Such action changes not only the initiand's physiology, but transforms her inner being as well.

This is seen in the Navajo practice of "molding" the kinaaldá girl, with the explicit intent of making the initiand attractive. As Frank Mitchell explained,

> The woman molds the girl to press her into a good figure and shape her body. At that time and period she is soft and can be pressed into certain forms. You shape her so she will have a good figure. If it is not done, she will probably have a belly like a nanny goat's. The present day has things such as beauty contests; there, girls are judged by the shape of their bodies. Just anyone can notice that in a crowd of people, you notice a perfect body right away. Others that are all out of shape also attract your eyes.[11]

It is a mistake, however, to take this statement at face value. In the first place, it does not account for the fact that it must be an ideal woman, model of all the virtues, who molds a kinaaldá girl, since the molder is expected to transmit her good qualities in the act of molding.[12] More important, it ignores a fundamental tenet of Navajo religion whereby the beautiful and the good are taken to be one and the same. Frisbie explains, with specific reference to the "molding":

> The girl is molded so she will be beautiful. Being beautiful in this case, however, implies more than having a good figure. It means the girl will be strong, ambitious, and capable of enduring much. The molding affects the girl's personality as well as her body. It implies that she will be friendly, unselfish, and cheerful; it means she will be a kind mother and a responsible housekeeper. A "beautiful" girl, therefore, is not only physically appealing; she is also "good" and "useful."[13]

It is not the girl's body that is transformed, but the girl herself. The same is true for the Tiv girl, who has the pattern of time placed upon her belly. The scars are not simply ornamental, nor are they the means of presenting certain eternal truths in symbolic form. If the latter were the case, the pattern might just as well be carved on a tree, molded in clay, or drawn on paper. It is essential, however, that the pattern be etched upon the initiand's body, for as her flesh is altered, so her very being is transformed as well, and the aim of this, as of all initiation, is transformation and not mere instruction.

Bodily mutation is also found in the Tukuna ritual, where the initiand's depilation is a high point of the ceremony. As among the Navajo, however, this theme is subordinated to another: identification with a goddess or mythical heroine. In the course of her initiation, the Navajo woman becomes Changing Woman and repeats the events of the goddess' Kinaaldá, which was the prototype of such ceremonies; the Tukuna initiand becomes Ariana, becomes the woman who survived the demons' attack, becomes the Mother of Timbó; and, if I am right in my reconstruction, certain Greek women became Persephone in the enactment of the Eleusinian Mysteries.

One clear goal of these rites is, of course, to appropriate the qualities of a goddess or heroine for the individual initiand. As Changing Woman was fruitful, so may she be fruitful; as Ariana was courageous, so may she have courage, and so forth. But beyond this, it must be noted that the figures with whom initiands are associated bear a striking similarity: each one served in some measure as a culture heroine, a bearer of civilizing gifts. Changing Woman and the Tukuna heroine were responsible for victories over monsters, demons, or forces of chaos; Changing Woman and Ariana brought corn to mankind; the Mother of Timbó brought forth an important drug; and Persephone's return coincided with the appearance of grain and agriculture. Persephone's return also prompted the foundation of the Mysteries, and the first Kinaaldá was established for Changing Woman. As each initiand assumes the role of these figures, the mythic events are repeated and the gifts of civilization reappropriated. Initiation thus is expected to benefit not only the individual initiand but society as a whole, and beyond this the entire cosmos.

In initiations where there is an identification with a mythic heroine, it is the initiand's temporal situation rather than her body that is the locus of change. When she takes on the role of a goddess, the initiand must abandon the historical moment in which she lives and enter the primordial, atemporal mode of existence characteristic of myth.[14] Her acts are no longer those of a specific woman at a specific point in time, limited in their range and power. They become the timeless acts of a divine being, ever repeated, ever renewed, infinite in their scope and eternal in duration. In becoming the goddess or culture heroine, the girl shatters the temporal restrictions of her own existence and becomes a being who is beyond death, beyond aging, beyond time. Furthermore, all those who participate in her initiation accompany her into the mythic atemporality. Those present at the all-night sing become the Holy People at Emergence Rim; guests at the Moça Nova festival become demons by means of masks; and the Eleusinian Mystai become Demeter, Iambe, Triptolemos, and others. At the moment of a girl's maturity, time is annihilated for her and for all those around her as they enter the world of myth, a world of absolute beginnings and thus rich in creative potential. To the extent that the initiand retains her identification with the goddess or heroine beyond the context of the ritual, she retains her creative power. Granted, she must reenter historical time at the ceremony's close, but one who has stepped outside time and become as the gods can never again be the same. The ideology is hardly so pedestrian as Driver would have it when he said of the Kinaaldá and other related rituals: "During the entire ceremony she [the initiand] impersonates a culture heroine in the hope that she will become as virtuous and successful."[15] The question is not one of impersonation, and virtue or success are the least of the ritual's goals. The girl *becomes* the goddess or culture heroine, and forever after her life partakes of the divine.

In initiations centering on a cosmic journey, the change that the initiand undergoes is conceived of as taking place in space rather than in time, as is true of the type of ritual involving identification with a mythic heroine (although the two types often overlap). But just as the goal of identification is to free the initiand from the limitations of existence at a single point in time, so that of the cosmic journey is to liberate her from the limitations of existence within a single house, village, or local area. A similar phenomenon can be observed in the travels of students within our own culture after graduation from high school or college. The goal is not so much "to see the world," however much that is the stated intent, as it is to shatter confining restrictions, to win and exercise freedom *in general,* spatial freedom being merely the way in which this broader freedom is most easily demonstrated. If such travels involve some danger (as, for instance, travel by hitchhiking), so much the better, for the mastery of such dangers demonstrates the ability to deal with the dimensions of existence unlocked by the exercise of freedom.

Such travel, however, is but a shadow of the travels expected of the initiand in such ceremonies as the Tukuna Moça Nova festival or what I assume to have been practiced in Greece on the basis of the Persephone myth. In these ceremonies young women left the land of the living, descended into the underworld, confronted the lord of the dead or a host of demonic creatures, and emerged victorious, bringing with them valuable gifts. The Tukuna woman journeyed to the heavens and beneath the seas, making a tour of the entire cosmos.

It is possible to view these journeys as ordeals, in which the initiand is tested and hardened, and it is also possible to see them as educational, teaching her more about the world than her previous confined life allowed her to learn. There is truth in both formulations, although neither is entirely adequate. The goal of initiation is not merely to make a better, stronger, or more knowledgeable person of the initiand, however much this may be desired, but to transform her utterly, make her totally different from what she had been, and radically separate her from her childhood existence. The cosmic journey makes the immature girl into a woman whose proper field of activity is the cosmos, who has transcended the bounds of her mundane existence and has become a truly cosmic being, jolted out of her immediate locale and introduced to the universe at large.

The type of initiation that centers on the play of opposites is more difficult to characterize than the other types. This is partly because it does not have a readily identifiable locus of action, and partly because it is more complex. It works along dialectical lines, presenting two contrasting entities and resolving their differences in a higher synthesis. Ultimately, the initiand is identified with this synthesis, partaking of its totality and stepping beyond the conflicts that characterize ordinary existence.

At first glance, it might seem that the opposition of male and female would be of central importance in rites of women's initiation of this type. In the Tiyyar ritual, for instance, male and female are repeatedly contrasted as the initiand is placed in juxtaposition with rice (signifying semen), and phallic implements such as arrows, pestles, and the tāli. The opposition of male and female is resolved when the tāli is placed on the initiand's throat, whereupon she becomes something new and radically different. No longer simply female, she becomes female endowed with male, woman with tāli, married woman. Instead of being merely one half of an opposition, she becomes a totality, mature, perfected, set beyond the tensions that characterize divided existence of any sort.

The opposition of male and female, however, is only one of many that appear, and it is no more basic or important than any of the others. In the Tiyyar rite, a contrast of heaven and earth is present, being resolved in the image of the cosmic tree. Rather than belonging exclusively to the terrestrial or celestial mode of being, the initiand passes beyond both at the culmination of her ceremony, to become a sustaining part of the entire cosmos. In the Navajo ritual there is a contrast between corn batter and corn cake, a contrast resolved in the full process of vegetative development: seed, plant, food, seed, and so forth.[16] What is important here is not any one of the steps, but the total unfolding of life, growth, death, and rebirth. As the kinaaldá girl becomes Changing Woman, she becomes part of—and at the same time responsible for—the entire process.

Tiv scarification posits such contrasts as line/circle, lineage/age-set, ancestors/descendants, and, most important, past/future. This last opposition is resolved in the emergence of a present moment that is capable of drawing on the past as it creates the future. The present thus understood is not a hairline between "was" and "yet-to-be," but a totality filled with history and potentiality, and it is in such a total present that the initiand stands.

Other contrasts and syntheses are often encountered: inside/outside, ancient/new, pure/impure, east/west, sun/moon, naked/clothed, and others more concrete in nature, such as husked rice/unhusked rice, mortar/pestle, turquoise/whiteshell, and so forth. It cannot rightly be said, as have most structuralist theoreticians, that the contents of these oppositions are devoid of significance. Yet the general form of opposition and resolution is undeniably far more important than any of the specific terms employed. Regardless of the specifics, the resolution of opposites always involves a move from separation to unity, tension to harmony, and limitation to totality. By becoming a part of this process, an immature girl—incomplete, and imperfect— becomes an adult, as the nature of her very being is radically transformed.

These four types of women's initiation ritual ought not be seen as fully separate categories. Nowhere do they exist in pristine form. Most ceremonies seem to draw on one of these themes for the bulk of their imagery and ideology, making use of some or all of the others at various moments during the ritual process. Although the Kinaaldá primarily focuses on identification with a mythic heroine, elements of bodily mutation (the "molding"), the play of opposites (the preparation of the corn cake), and the cosmic journey (the girl's races to the east) are apparent. The Tukuna rite is primarily of the cosmic-journey type, including a series of identifications with mythic heroines and one clear moment of bodily mutation (depilation). The Tiyyar Tālikettukalyānam centers primarily on the play of opposites, with one moment of cosmic journey (the procession to the cosmic tree). Tiv scarification is of the bodily mutation type, with elements of the play of opposites. Lastly, if the Eleusinian Mysteries were practiced as I have suggested, they included an initiation almost equally rooted in cosmic journey and identification with a mythic heroine, the play of opposites also being involved at several points (above/below, famine/abundance, mourning/rejoicing, and so on).

So much for typology, but what of morphology? In these differing types, can a similar structure be perceived? That it can is the classic argument of Arnold van Gennep's *Rites de Passage,* in which he maintained not only that all initiatory rites but all rites that change an individual's social status conform to one basic pattern: a three-stage process whereby one is separated from one's previous environment (rites of separation or "pre-liminal" rites), spends a period of time in limbo ("liminal" or transition rites), and assumes a new station in life (rites of reincorporation, reaggregation, or "post-liminal" rites). Although some have maintained that this is nothing more than the observation that all actions have a beginning, middle and end, there is a good deal more subtlety in van Gennep's formulation.

The starting point for van Gennep's work is his perception that all rites of passage—initiations, weddings, funerals, births, and so forth—have as their "essential purpose" enabling the individual "to pass from one defined position to another which is equally well defined."[17] What is meant by this "defined position" is in almost all instances what we would refer to as a social status. Although van Gennep stated at one point that rituals might effect passage "from one cosmic or social world to another,"[18] the first half of this suggestion—which is extremely appropriate for women's initiations—is never pursued, and change in social rank occupies his attention almost exclusively. Between any two well-defined social positions, he argues, there lies a no-man's land, a liminal period during which one has lost a previously held status without yet having gained a new one to replace it. For the duration of this liminal period, which may last for months or years, one is without a status of any sort, and enjoying freedom from normal social restrictions, but also being subject to dangers normally protected against by society.[19]

In order to describe rites of passage, van Gennep often makes use of a spatial model, devoting an entire chapter to "the Territorial Passage," wherein he compares travel between well-defined territories via an ill-defined no-man's land to the logic of an initiation or other similar rite.[20] His language is full of spatial terms—"border," "threshold," "position," "passage"—and for him these have more than metaphorical meaning, for he argues that the rites of passage themselves make use of this spatial language. In his concluding remarks he stresses this as one of the most important points of his analysis, along with the typical order of rites of passage and the existence of the liminal stage:

> Third, it seems important to me that the passage from one social position to another is identified with a *territorial passage,* such as the entrance into a village or a house, the movement from one room to another, or the crossing of streets and squares. This identification explains why the passage from one group to another is so often ritually expressed by passage under a portal, or by an "opening of the doors." These phrases and events are seldom meant as "symbols"; for the semicivilized the passage is actually a territorial passage . . . In short, a change of social categories involves a change of residence, and this fact is expressed by the rites of passage in their various forms.[21]

With regard to initiatory ritual, this is perhaps clearest in rites such as men's initiation among the Australian peoples, where initiands are carried away from their dwellings (separation) into the bush, where they are subjected to various ordeals and given religious instruction (liminal rites), after which they are returned to their families, who receive them as adults or even as those risen from the dead (reincorporation). The three-part schema is thus graphically acted out in spatial terms: from the initiand's normal terrain to wilderness, and back to his normal terrain again, with a new status on returning. Male initiations frequently conform to this pattern, but van Gennep cites very few examples of women's initiations,[22] and the examples we have considered above point to a very different use of spatial language, which—if, with van Gennep, we are to take spatial language as more than a symbol or metaphor—reflects a different ritual structure and a different understanding of what initiation accomplishes.

In the first place, we look in vain for a spatial expression of separation in any of the rites we have considered, with the possible exception of the hypothesized reenactment of the Persephone myth, on which only conjecture is possible. The Tiv woman never leaves her mother's side and stays entirely within the bounds of her village, while Tiyyar, Navajo and Tukuna initiands spend their time of seclusion—what might be called their "liminal" periods—inside their family dwellings. While this may be a time of isolation (as with the Tukuna) or of restricted social contacts (as with the Navajo), it cannot rightly be called a separation: the initiand is not removed from the space that she normally inhabits. Only the nature of her activity is changed, not her spatial locus. Although there are, of course, examples of male initiation in which true separation does not occur and examples of female initiation in which it figures prominently, it seems to be much more closely correlated to the men's rites. Such a state of affairs has important theoretical repercussions.

Without a clear enactment of separation, one might question whether there can truly be a liminal period or a process of reincorporation, for nothing has been left behind and there is nowhere to which one can return. Thus, although women's initiations regularly conform to a three-part structure, the three stages cannot accurately be described as separation, liminality, reincorporation. Something different seems to be at work, and in place of van Gennep's terms I would suggest three others: enclosure, metamorphosis (or magnification), and emergence.

I am struck, for instance, by the metaphor of insect metamorphosis employed by the Tukuna to describe the Moça Nova festival: the initiand is likened to a caterpillar, who enters the cocoon and emerges a butterfly. The seclusion chamber is her chrysalis, where she acquires her new mode of being. The same might be said of the Tiyyar pandal and ancestral home, or of the Navajo hogan.

The importance of this shift in terminology can be perceived by recalling a remark in van Gennep's summary: "A change of social categories involves a change of residence."[23] In a great many women's initiations no such change of residence takes place, and herein lies one key for understanding the ways in which male and female initiations differ. The lack of any true separation from one's former dwelling space is due, I submit, to the fact that women do not have open to them a variety of sociopolitical statuses through which they may pass by means of initiation.

To be sure, women's lives involve a number of differentiated stages such as girl, marriageable woman, wife, mother, and so forth, but none of these carries significant weight in the sociopolitical arena of men. Women may be intimately involved in status distinctions within a domestic hierarchy, in which, for instance, a mother-in-law is set above her daughters-in-law or a senior wife is set above junior wives, but these distinctions have few ramifications beyond the immediate household. Ironically, the one point at which some societies permit women a small measure of sociopolitical status is when they are old and past the age of childbearing, at which time they are no longer classified as women.

For the most part, throughout history and throughout the cultures of the world, the social and political status of woman has not been her own, but only a reflection of the status of some male relative, most frequently her father, husband, or son. The consequences of this are far-reaching, and better elucidated in the feminist literature than in the ethnographic,[24] but one important result is that woman per se has no status. Status is the concern of the male, and women are excluded from direct participation in the social hierarchy. The only status that is independently theirs, if status it be, is that of woman.

The term "status" is somewhat vague within the context of (male) *rites de passage*, and in its place Meyer Fortes has suggested "office," a word that strikes me as particularly apt in view of its connotations of power, authority, and prestige.[25] It is also abundantly clear that women are universally barred from "office," and initiation nowhere confers upon them new sociopolitical power or prestige. It is noteworthy that both van Gennep and Fortes offer the same impoverished view of women's initiations, seeing as their dominant or sole purpose the transition of an individual from an asexual world to the world of sexuality.[26] This, in van Gennep's opinion, is due to the fact that "the social activity of a woman is much simpler than that of a man."[27]

This contrast between what initiation accomplishes for men and what it accomplishes for women is graphically presented in the spatial terms of their respective rituals. For men, initiation is an installation to office, a change from one level of authority and responsibility to a higher one, and as such it involves a spatial transition or change in residence. For women, no such installation is possible: a woman remains always a woman, no office is open to her, and thus her initiation involves no spatial change. She remains where she has always been, in terms of hierarchy as well as domicile, and this is why she is secluded within her normal living space, rather than separated from it at the outset of initiation.

The preceding analysis bears directly on whether van Gennep's notion of liminality is applicable to women's initiations, for there exists a curious inverse relation between social hierarchy and the liminal state, as Victor Turner has argued.[28] Using the example of neophytes in initiation, Turner has emphasized that they are regularly stripped of property, insignia, and clothing during the liminal stage, so that all initiands stand equal to one another, having been "reduced or ground down to a uniform condition."[29] Turner notes that "among themselves, neophytes tend to develop an intense comradeship and egalitarianism. Secular distinctions of rank and status disappear or are homogenized."[30] This state of comradeship, homogeneity, lack of individual differentiation and social hierarchy he calls "communitas," and he sees it as the hallmark of the liminal state. Communitas develops when social structure is dissolved, an event that permits a "communion of equal individuals" to emerge.[31] "For me," Turner says, "communitas emerges where social structure is not."[32]

There are difficulties in applying this set of ideas to women's initiation, however, for women cannot be truly said to be a part of the social hierarchy, or to have any significant independent status. Never having such status, they cannot be deprived of it, and one is forced to conclude either that there can be no liminal state for women or that women exist always in a liminal state.[33] In either event, it is not initiation that introduces women to a world devoid of status distinctions.

The difference between men's and women's initiation in this regard is perhaps suggested by the contrasting ways in which they employ the symbolism of clothes and nudity. Turner emphasizes one possible set of clothing symbolism, a set commonly found in male rites:

> Liminal entities, such as neophytes in initiation or puberty rites, may be represented as possessing nothing. They may be disguised as monsters, wear only a strip of clothing, or even go naked, to demonstrate that as liminal beings they have no status, property, insignia, secular clothing indicating rank or role, position in a kinship system—in short, nothing that may distinguish them from their fellow neophytes or initiands.[34]

In the female rites we have studied, however, the symbolism of clothing is entirely different. Instead of the removal of clothing, we find the addition of new clothing or bodily adornment—a marriage token, a feather headdress, elaborate jewelry, or a set of scars. Attendants deck the initiand in ceremonial finery, often piling layer upon layer, as among the Tukuna or the Navajo. The general tendency in women's rites seems to be toward an additive process (clothes put on) rather than a subtractive one (clothes taken off). This serves to express another contrast with male initiations: whereas men (who have a status) must lose their status in order to assume another, women (who have no status) need not do so. For them there is no true liminality, no stress on nudity,[35] no "being ground down to nothing." Their initiation proceeds along quite different lines.

Rather than changing women's status, initiation changes their fundamental being, addressing ontological concerns rather than hierarchical ones. A woman does not become more powerful or authoritative, but more creative, more alive, more ontologically real. Insofar as one can never fully be deprived of one's essential being in the way that one can be stripped of status or office, there can be no period in absolute limbo. The pattern of female initiation is thus one of growth or magnification, an expansion of powers, capabilities, experiences. This magnification is accomplished by gradually endowing the initiand with symbolic items that make of her a woman, and beyond this a cosmic being. These items can be concrete, such as clothing or jewelry, or they can be nonmaterial in nature, such as songs chanted for the woman-to-be, myths repeated in her presence, scars or paintings placed upon her body.

Tiv scarification provides a good example of this process of magnification. Charles Keil writes of scarification as an "intensive" experience, meaning this "in the sense of intense pain endured and an enduring record of that pain presented at all times thereafter. The person scarified is intensified, augmented; his or her personal characteristics are further specialized, rendered unique. The marks must not only fit personal body shapes, but the shape of a growing personality that will command the center of attention."[36]

The Tiyyar example is also instructive. From the time her initiation begins, the initiand symbolically experiences menstruation by means of her seclusion as if for menarche; marriage through the tying of the tāli; defloration through her puncturing the leaf over the divinatory pot; pregnancy through the objects hidden within the pot; childbirth through the extraction of one of these objects; lactation through the seat made of milkwood. In these actions she experiences certain crucial moments of a woman's life, and in so doing becomes a woman. She also receives a number of items that represent male existence: rice, arrows, and the tāli. If the symbols drawn from a woman's life cycle amplify her being and make of her a woman, these male symbols provide further magnification, transforming her into a total, perfected being, beyond the divisions and limitations of sexuality. As such, she is really more than human; she has passed beyond the bounds of finite terrestrial existence, and with further magnification she steps into the cosmic arena: she is given the water of life, with which she nourishes the cosmic tree.

There is a limit to such magnification, however, and ultimately a matured individual must leave the chrysalis behind. The emergence of the initiand from seclusion stands as the culminating moment in four of the five rites we have examined. The Tiyyar woman leads a procession from the pandal to the foot of the cosmic tree; the Navajo comes from the hogan to serve her corn cake; the Tukuna, her seclusion chamber cut apart like a cocoon, steps out to face assaulting demons and tour the universe; and the Greek woman who played the part of Persephone seems to have emerged from the Anaktoron in a blaze of light, revealing herself to the assembled Mystai. When these initiands come forth, they are ready to sustain life—not only their own, but that of their people and the cosmos as well.

The ultimate claim—that a woman's initiation and a woman's subsequent life have cosmic significance—is regularly made, either implicitly or explicitly, and its importance cannot be overestimated. The initiand is regarded as having become a deity, a culture heroine, a sacred object, the tender of the cosmic tree, the link between past and future. In contrast to the sociopolitical status regularly conferred by men's initiations, women's rites bestow a cosmic status, a defined place in the universe, and a place of importance and dignity.[37]

Rituals of women's initiation commonly include three closely related claims. They claim to transform a girl into a woman, and this they clearly accomplish, by definition if by no other test: after initiation one is never again considered a girl. They claim to renew society, and this too they accomplish, first by providing society with a new productive member, and second by bringing the social totality together for a joyous celebration. Lastly they claim to renew the cosmos, and the validity of this audacious claim is somewhat harder to assess.

The reasons why the cosmic claim is advanced, however, can be discerned in the teleology of the ritual—its desired results, implicit as well as explicit, and also the means it adopts toward these ends, which is to say, its strategy. Two points that emerged from our previous discussion are particularly useful in assessing this strategy. First, women's lives permit no significant change in sociopolitical status such as that which is open to men. Second, women's initiations stress the cosmic rather than the social dimensions of existence. These points are closely related, and suggest that the strategy of women's initiation is to lead a woman's life (and, *a fortiori*, her attention) away from the sociopolitical arena, introducing her to the real or imagined splendors of the cosmos instead. To put it in different terms, women's initiation offers a religious compensation for a sociopolitical deprivation. Or, to put it differently still, it is an opiate for an oppressed class.

Debarred from office, excluded from positions in which independent power may legitimately be exercised, confined to the lowest social statuses, women have never had an easy time of it in any culture that has ever existed. Despite the ill-founded theories of Bachofen and others concerning a primordial "Mutterrecht," it is now clear that nowhere have women ever held effective sociopolitical power.[38] Women's initiation does not contest this state of affairs. It is a ritual enacted by society as a whole, and like all rituals performed by the social totality, it serves to preserve the social status quo. There is nothing revolutionary in women's initiation; it serves only to introduce an individual into society as society already exists, not to alter the nature of that society. Cosmic claims notwithstanding, the desired result of the ritual is to make a girl ready and willing to assume the traditional place of a woman as defined within a given culture. Such a place may be none too attractive, and yet the ritual succeeds with only the rarest of exceptions. Anne Keith interviewed a number of young Navajo women who had just celebrated their Kinaaldá. Their responses highlighted the way in which the ritual prepared them for a woman's labor. "Well," said one of the women, "if you're cheerful four days maybe you get the habit of it, doing it all your life. And if you put the food before the people all the time and try to help around the house, you'll be willing to do those things for the people wherever you go . . . You know, when you grow up, you got to learn sometime. You get most of those things out of those four days. As a woman. I mean most of the things you got to do as a mother."[39] Sung over, celebrated, assimilated to the goddess, she is now ready to take up her chores. The strategy is that of placing woman on a pedestal, carried to its outermost possibilities: speak of her as a goddess to make of her a drudge.

These rituals, however, can be viewed from a different and equally valid perspective. Returning to Keith's informants, another young woman was asked what would happen if a girl didn't have the Kinaaldá celebrated for her, to which she replied, "If you don't do that, you won't learn how to do *anything*."[40] The emphasis on learning is of particular interest here, for, as Keith pointed out, there is virtually nothing of a practical nature that is taught or learned within the Kinaaldá: "Since pre-adolescent girls do a lot of these jobs in many families, they are not learning *new* skills; and the ceremony is, instead, stressing the *importance* of the skills in every Navajo woman's life."[41] Even a stronger statement could be made: it is not just the *importance* of the skills that is communicated, but the fact that they are filled with cosmic significance, thoroughly imbued with transcendent meaning. While Keith points out that most recent initiands are relatively ignorant of the deeper aspects of the Kinaaldá, she also stresses that the two things they do know are the nature of Changing Woman and the fact that the first Kinaaldá was performed for her. That is, they realize that throughout the ritual they are repeating the paradigmatic acts of their divine ancestress.[42]

It is rare that a ritual can alter the basic ways in which society is organized. Nor do rituals shape the way in which people live so much as they shape the way people understand the lives they would lead in any event. A hunter must hunt, whether his hunting is accompanied by rituals or not. An agriculturalist must till the soil, and no ritual compels him to do so. What rituals can do is to transform necessary activities from unremitting drudgery into something rich, satisfying, and filled with meaning. Ritual thus makes hunting or planting into sacred activities by defining them as repetitions of divine primordial gestures or acts necessary to preserve the cosmic order. In this way, ritual makes it possible for people to derive profound emotional and intellectual satisfaction from otherwise pedestrian affairs, because it points to something cosmic, transcendent, or sacred concealed within the tedium of mundane existence.

The crucial function of women's initiation is similar, in that it endows the lives of women with a sense of meaning and dignity, their sociopolitical disfranchisement notwithstanding. In general, rituals do not focus on the emptiest aspects of people's lives, but on those aspects that are most full. In rites of initiation it is women's creativity that occupies center stage: their role as bearer of young, raiser of crops, provider of food, sustainer of life.

This is not merely an extension of the understanding that women become capable of giving birth as a result of initiation. Winning individual fertility is but the tip of the iceberg, and here one must again confront the cosmic claim encountered in women's initiations. For through the process of symbolic amplification, a woman's individual fertility is redefined in ever grander terms, ultimately merging with the idea of creativity in its broadest possible form: cosmic creativity. The Tiv woman does not simply gain the ability to reproduce, but becomes the guarantor of her family's continuity, her people's continuity, and, in the last analysis, the continuity of time, for were it not for her creativity there would be no future to succeed the past. Neither is the Navajo woman's creativity limited to bearing children. Having become Changing Woman, it is she who makes the crops come up, she who makes the seasons change, she who ensures the victory of the Holy People over monsters and chaos. In these and other instances, such as the Tiyyar, Tukuna, and Greek rituals, the initiand begins as a person on whom no one depends, and through the course of initiation becomes one on whom the welfare of the entire cosmos hinges. Each time a woman is initiated, the world is saved from chaos, for the fundamental power of creativity is renewed in her being.

It is at this point that the distinction commonly made between rituals performed for the benefit of an individual, the so-called "rites of passage," and those performed for the benefit of the world, the so-called "rites of cosmic maintenance," breaks down. Women's initiation is performed for the benefit of the initiand, of society, and of the cosmos. No doubt the benefit is greatest for the initiand, who becomes in her own mind and that of others a goddess, a sacred object, and so forth—identifications that she will carry with her beyond the ritual context and that will infuse all her future actions with meaning. Society benefits because it gains a new productive member, and there are broader benefits as well. Those in attendance have their feeling of solidarity—the sentiment that holds society together—renewed by their participation in the rite, and, what is more, they come away with a restored sense that there is meaning in existence, in their own lives as in that of the initiand.

Such a sense of meaning is the greatest benefit that any ritual can bestow, and it is the ultimate function of all ritual to invest life with a deeper meaning than animal survival. A sense of meaning elevates life above boredom, mindlessness, and despair. It makes even the harshest existence worthwhile and bestows dignity on all of one's actions, however trivial they might otherwise seem. Whether the cosmos is renewed as a result, as is claimed within rites of women's initiation, is difficult for us to assess. But one can certainly say that a world in which individuals and societies find meaning in creative action is a very different world from one in which this has ceased to be the case. To this extent, rituals do live up to their claims, and the universe is made richer by their faithful performance.

Analysis of the cosmic claim leads to contradictory results. On the one hand, the notion that the universe is renewed through the initiation of a woman can be seen as an opiate, a comforting and intoxicating fantasy provided for those who will never be granted power or position. Viewed thus, it is a cynical lie, an opportunistic stratagem that functions to preserve male hegemony. No romantic appreciation for the depth and beauty of women's initiations should keep us from seeing their darker side.

We would be equally misled, however, were we to mistake the dark side for the total phenomenon. The cosmic claim is not just a lie, however much it may be one from a materialist perspective. It is also the means whereby the lives of individual women take on meaning, and one method whereby meaning is introduced into the world. This is ultimately the most profound claim that any ritual or any religious system can make: that through their thoughts and actions, people can fill their existence with meaning.

Ritual spans both these poles—the materialist and the romantic— and no interpretation that is faithful to the data can afford to overlook either one. Women's initiation is a highly ambiguous rite. To put it in extreme terms, it is simultaneously a ritual of sacrifice and an apotheosis, with the initiand at once the community's lamb-led-to-slaughter and its deity-in-the-making. Both elements are equally real, equally important, and equally worthy of our attention. No analysis that minimizes either the romantic side or the materialist side can be accurate or complete. As students of ritual we cannot be taken in by strategic deceptions, nor can we allow the materialism of our own culture to anesthetize us to other dimensions of existence.

Notes

1. INTRODUCTION

1. The most important work in recent years is, of course, Victor Turner, *The Ritual Process* (Chicago: Aldine, 1969), a brilliant extension and elaboration of the theories of Arnold van Gennep, *The Rites of Passage*, tr. M. B. Vizedom and G. L. Caffee (1908; Chicago: University of Chicago Press, 1960), [French edition: 1908], drawing heavily on Turner's own fieldwork among the Ndembu of central Africa.

2. On paleolithic evidence, see the summary discussion in Mircea Eliade, *Histoire des croyances et des idées religieuses*, vol. 1 (Paris: Payot, 1976), pp. 13–39, with citation of the relevant literature. On animal behavior, see the important set of papers presented at the conference organized by Sir Julian Huxley on the topic of "Ritualization of Behavior in Animals and Man," in *Philosophical Transactions of the Royal Society*, ser. B, vol. 251 (1966).

3. See the example cited in the preface.

4. On movies: Mircea Eliade, *Myths, Dreams, and Mysteries* (New York: Harper and Row, 1960), pp. 34f. On greetings: Herbert Fingarette, *Confucius—The Secular as Sacred* (New York: Harper and Row, 1972), pp. 9–11. On footnotes: Bruce Lincoln, "Two Notes on Modern Rituals," *Journal of the American Academy of Religion* 45 (1977): 152–155. On this whole topic, see the essays collected in Sally F. Moore and Barbara Myerhoff, *Secular Ritual: Forms and Meanings* (Assen: van Gorcum, 1977).

5. Edmund R. Leach, "Ritual," in *International Encyclopedia of the Social Sciences*, vol. 13 (New York: Macmillan, 1968), pp. 523f; idem, *Culture and Communication* (Cambridge: Cambridge University Press, 1976), pp. 37–45.

6. Johan Huizinga, *Homo Ludens* (Boston: Beacon, 1950), pp. 14ff.

7. Adolf E. Jensen, *Myth and Cult among Primitive Peoples* (Chicago: University of Chicago Press, 1963), esp. p. 132.

8. See the essays collected in Richard Schechner and Mady Schuman, eds., *Ritual, Play, and Performance* (New York: Seabury Press, 1976).

9. Max Gluckman, "Les Rites de Passage," in Max Gluckman, ed., *Essays on the Ritual of Social Relations* (Manchester: Manchester University Press, 1962), pp. 26ff.

10. This is the general position of the "Myth and Ritual" school, whose

theories have appeared in S. H. Hooke, ed., *Myth and Ritual* (London: Oxford University Press, 1933); idem, ed., *Myth, Ritual and Kingship* (Oxford: Clarendon Press, 1958); and idem, ed., *The Labyrinth* (New York: Macmillan, 1935).

11. R. R. Marett, *The Threshold of Religion*, 2nd ed. (London: Methuen, 1914), p. 181.

12. A. R. Radcliffe-Brown, *Structure and Function in Primitive Society* (London: Cohen and West, 1952), p. 157.

13. Roger Caillois, *L'Homme et le sacré* (Paris: Presses Universitaires de France, 1939), pp. 88ff.

14. Konrad Lorenz, "The Psychobiological Approach," in Huxley, "Ritualization of Behavior in Animals and Man," p. 279.

15. Roy A. Rappaport, *Pigs for the Ancestors* (New Haven: Yale University Press, 1968), esp. pp. 1–4.

16. Theodor Reik, *Ritual: Psychoanalytic Studies* (London: Hogarth Press, 1931), pp. 15ff.

17. Henri Hubert and Marcel Mauss, *Sacrifice: Its Nature and Function*, tr. W. D. Halls (Chicago: University of Chicago Press, 1964), esp. p. 97.

18. Mircea Eliade, *The Myth of the Eternal Return* (Princeton: Princeton University Press, 1954), esp. p. 76.

19. This refusal to become embroiled in methodological and definitional disputes, together with an insistence on confronting primary sources, has made possible the deep and probing examination of Indian mythology by Wendy Doniger O'Flaherty, *Asceticism and Eroticism in the Mythology of Siva* (Oxford: Oxford University Press, 1973); idem, *The Origins of Evil in Hindu Mythology* (Berkeley: University of California Press, 1976).

20. Hebraic and Vedic sacrifices formed the basis of Hubert and Mauss, *Sacrifice: Its Origin and Function*, one of the most influential works ever written on ritual, and consideration of Hebraic sacrifice led to the theories of W. Robertson Smith, *Lectures on the Religion of the Semites*, 2nd ed. (London: A. and C. Black, 1894), another extraordinarily influential work. The totemic meal lies at the heart of the theories of Sigmund Freud, *Totem and Taboo*, tr. A. A. Brill (New York: Vintage, 1918); and Emile Durkheim, *The Elementary Forms of the Religious Life*, tr. J. W. Swain (New York: Free Press, 1915). On Nemi, see Sir James George Frazer, *The Golden Bough*, 3rd ed., 12 vols. (London: Macmillan, 1907–1912).

21. New Year's ceremonies: This is true for Vittorio Lanternari, *La Grande Festa* (Bari: Dedalo, 1976), and for the entire "Myth and Ritual" school cited above, including also Ivan Engnell, *Studies in Divine Kingship in the Ancient Near East* (Uppsala: Almquist and Wiksells, 1943); Theodor H. Gaster, *Thespis* (New York: Harper and Row, 1961); Eliade, *Myth of the Eternal Return;* and others. Australian ceremonies are the crucial examples used by van Gennep in the central chapter of *The Rites of Passage*, that on initiation. This chapter (pp. 65–115), which is almost twice as long as any other chapter (betrothal and marriage—30 pp.; funerals—20 pp.; birth and childhood—15 pp.; pregnancy and childbirth—9 pp.), provided the clearest and most telling examples for van Gennep's famous pattern of separation /liminality/reintegration. Significantly, the Australian data stand at the head of the chapter, and just before writing *Les Rites de passage* van Gennep had published two studies based entirely on Australian materials: *Mythes et légendes d'Australie* (Paris: E. Guilmoto, 1906); and *Desseins sur peaux d'opossum australiennes* (The Hague: Rijks Ethnographisch Museum, 1907).

Australian examples also figure prominently in Mircea Eliade, *Rites and Symbols of Initiation* (New York: Harper and Row, 1958).

22. Most notably, W. O. E. Oesterley, *The Sacred Dance* (Cambridge: Cambridge University Press, 1923); G. van der Leeuw, *In dem Himmel ist ein Tanz* (Munich: G. Ullmann, 1943); and Phillipe de Félice, *L'Enchantement des danses et la magie du verbe* (Paris: A. Michel, 1957).

23. See the essays collected in Ari Kiev, *Magic, Faith, and Healing* (Glencoe: Free Press, 1964).

24. Victor and Edith Turner, *Image and Pilgrimage in Christian Culture: Anthropological Perspectives* (New York: Columbia University Press, 1978).

25. André Caquat and Marcel Leibovici, eds., *La Divination* (Paris: Presses Universitaires de France, 1968); William Bascom, *Ifa Divination* (Bloomington: Indiana University Press, 1969); Evan Zuesse, "Divination and Deity in African Religions," *History of Religions* 15 (1975): 158–182.

26. Frank W. Young, *Initiation Ceremonies: A Cross-Cultural Study of Status Dramatization* (Indianapolis: Bobbs-Merrill, 1965), p. 15, reports that of the one hundred cultures he sampled, 57 percent practiced women's initiation and only 40 percent practiced men's, although he considers the latter more "dramatized" (p. 18).

27. The most important works on the topic of initiation remain van Gennep, *The Rites of Passage*, esp. pp. 65–115; and Eliade, *Rites and Symbols of Initiation*. In addition, one should note C. J. Bleeker, ed., *Initiation* (Leiden: E. J. Brill, 1965); Vittorio Maçoni, *L'iniziazione tribale* (Genoa: Tilgher, 1973); Felix Speiser, "Über Initiationen in Australien und Neuguinea," *Verhandlungen der naturforschenden Gesellschaft in Basel* (1929), pp. 56–258; Adolf E. Jensen, *Beschneidung und Reifezeremonien bei Naturvölker* (Stuttgart: Strecker und Schroeder, 1932); Richard Thurnwald, "Primitive Initiations—und Wiedergeburtsriten," *Eranos Jahrbuch* 7 (1939): 321–398; and Goblet d'Alviella, "L'Initiation: Institution sociale, magique et religieuse," *Revue de l'Histoire des Religions* 81 (1920): 1–28.

Specifically psychological theories of initiation have appeared in Theodor Reik, "The Puberty Rites of Savages," in *Ritual: Psychoanalytic Studies*, pp. 91–166; idem, *The Creation of Woman* (New York: George Braziller, 1960); idem, *The Temptation* (New York: George Braziller, 1961); Moritz Zeller, *Die Knabenweihen: Ein psychologisch-ethnologische Studie* (Bern: P. Haupt, 1923); Joseph L. Henderson, *Thresholds of Initiation* (Middletown, Conn.: Wesleyan University Press, 1967); and Bruno Bettelheim, *Symbolic Wounds: Puberty Rites and the Envious Male* (New York: Collier, 1962).

Theories that are sociological in their orientation include: John W. M. Whiting, Richard Kluckhohn, and Albert Anthony, "The Function of Male Initiation Ceremonies at Puberty," in Eleanor E. Maccoby et al., eds., *Readings in Social Psychology* (New York: Holt, Rinehart and Winston, 1958), pp. 359–370; Yehudi A. Cohen, *The Transition from Childhood to Adolescence* (Chicago: Aldine, 1964); M. R. Allen, *Male Cults and Secret Initiations in Melanesia* (Melbourne: Melbourne University Press, 1967); V. Popp, ed., *Initiation: Zeremonien der Status Änderung und des Rollenwechsels* (Frankfurt: Suhrkamp, 1969); Young, *Initiation Ceremonies: A Cross-Cultural Study of Status Dramatization;* and Brian M. Du Toit, *Configurations of Cultural Continuity* (Rotterdam: A. A. Balkema, 1976).

With specific regard to rites of women's initiation, two outstanding case studies should be noted: Audrey I. Richards, *Chisungu: A Girls' Initiation Ceremony among the Bemba of Northern Rhodesia* (London: Faber and Faber,

1956); and Victor Turner, *The Drums of Affliction* (Oxford: Clarendon Press, 1968), pp. 198–268. Others include Peter Rigby, "The Structural Context of Girls' Puberty Rites," *Man* 2 (1967): 434–444; Alice Schlegel, "The Adolescent Socialization of the Hopi Girl," *Ethnology* 12 (1973): 449–462; and J. S. La Fontaine, "Ritualization of Women's Life-Crises in Bugisu," in J. S. La Fontaine, ed., *The Interpretation of Ritual: Essays in Honour of A. I. Richards* (London: Tavistock, 1972), pp. 159–186. I know of only two theoretical studies: D. Visca, "Le iniziazioni femminili: Un problema da riconsiderare," *Religioni e Civilta* 2 (1976); and Judith K. Brown, "A Cross-Cultural Study of Female Initiation Rites," *American Anthropologist* 65 (1973): 837–853. Brown's findings have been accepted by Peter Kloos, "Female Initiation among the Maroni River Caribs," *American Anthropologist* 71 (1969): 898–905; and Morris E. Opler, "Cause and Effect in Apachean Agriculture, Division of Labor, Residence Patterns, and Girls' Puberty Rites," *American Anthropologist* 74 (1972): 1133–46; but contested by Harold E. Driver, "Girls' Puberty Rites and Matrilocal Residence," *American Anthropologist* 71 (1969): 905–908; idem, "Reply to Opler on Apachean Subsistence, Residence, and Girls' Puberty Rites," *American Anthropologist* 74 (1972): 1147–51. See also Harold E. Driver, "Girls' Puberty Rites in Western North America," *University of California Publications in Anthropological Records* 6 (1941): 21–90.

28. As reported in Marcel Griaule, *Conversations with Ogotemmeli* (London: Oxford University Press, 1965), pp. 22 and 158ff; Otto Meinardus, "Mythological, Historical, and Sociological Aspects of the Practice of Female Circumcision among the Egyptians," *Acta Ethnographica* 16 (1967): 387–397.

29. Rose Oldfield Hayes, "Female Genital Mutilation, Fertility Control, Women's Roles, and the Patrilineage in Modern Sudan: A Functional Analysis," *American Ethnologist* 2 (1975): 617–633.

30. Note such unsatisfactory accounts as P. Vorman, "Initiationsfeiern der Jünglinge und Mädchen bei den Monumbo-Papua," *Anthropos* 10 (1915): 178–179; Camilla H. Wedgwood, "Girls' Puberty Rites in Manam Island, New Guinea," *Oceania* 4 (1933): 132–155; J. Whiteman, "Girls' Puberty Ceremonies among the Chimbu," *Anthropos* 60 (1965): 410–422; John Alan Ross, "The Puberty Ceremony of the Chimbu Girl," *Anthropos* 60 (1965): 423–432.

31. On women's rituals in Australia, see: Geza Róheim, "Women and Their Life in Central Australia," *Journal of the Royal Anthropological Institute* 63 (1933): 207–267; Phyllis M. Kaberry, *Aboriginal Woman: Sacred and Profane* (London: George Routledge, 1939): pp. 99, 230ff; Roland M. and Catherine H. Berndt, *The World of the First Australians* (Chicago: University of Chicago Press, 1964), pp. 150–157; and Jane Goodale, *Tiwi Wives* (Seattle: University of Washington Press, 1971), pp. 204–214. Male Australian materials provide the starting point for most studies of initiation: van Gennep, pp. 74–76; Eliade, *Rites and Symbols of Initiation*, pp. 4–20; Turnwald, pp. 330–356; Bettelheim, pp. 85ff, 93ff, 100ff, 120ff, 134ff, 161ff, et passim; and Speiser, the last of whom considered only evidence from Australia and New Guinea.

32. On the ability of symbols to produce change, see, inter alia, Claude Lévi-Strauss, "The Effectiveness of Symbols," *Structural Anthropology* (Garden City, N.Y.: Doubleday, 1963), pp. 181–201; and M. Esther Hardin, "What Makes the Symbol Effective as a Healing Agent," in Gerhard

Adler, ed., *Current Trends in Analytical Psychology* (London: Tavistock, 1961), pp. 1–18.

33. John Gillin, "Magical Fright," in William Lessa and Evon Z. Vogt, *Reader in Comparative Religion* (New York: Harper and Row, 1958), p. 361.

34. Meyer Fortes, "Ritual and Office in Tribal Society," in Gluckman, *Essays on the Ritual of Social Relations*, p. 68.

2. TĀLIKETTUKALYĀNAM

1. The tāli is so common a token of marriage that it has been compared to the Western wedding ring. See Edgar Thurston, *Ethnographic Notes in Southern India* (Madras: Government Press, 1906), p. 1n; and Anantha Krishna Iyer, *Lectures on Ethnography* (Calcutta: University of Calcutta, 1925), p. 161.

2. Kathleen Gough, "Tiyyar: North Kerala," in David M. Schneider and Kathleen Gough, eds., *Matrilineal Kinship* (Berkeley: University of California Press, 1961), p. 410; "The Nayars and the Definition of Marriage," *Journal of the Royal Anthropological Institute* 89 (1959): 25f; M. S. A. Rao, *Social Change in Malabar* (Bombay: Popular Press, 1957), pp. 79f, 86, and 93.

3. See E. Kathleen Gough, "Female Initiation Rites on the Malabar Coast," *Journal of the Royal Anthropological Institute* 85 (1955): 45–80.

4. For a psychoanalytic interpretation, see Gough, "Female Initiation Rites," esp. pp. 62–78. For a sociological view, see Louis Dumont, "Les Mariages Nayar comme faits indiens," *L'Homme* 1 (1961): 11–36; and Nur Yalman, "On the Purity of Women in the Castes of Ceylon and Malabar," *Journal of the Royal Anthropological Institute* 93 (1963): 25–58. For a structuralist perspective, see Edmund Leach, "A Critique of Yalman's Interpretation of Sinhalese Girl's Puberty Ceremonial," in Jean Pouillon and Pierre Maranda, eds., *Echanges et Communications: Mélanges offerts à Claude Lévi-Strauss* (The Hague: Mouton, 1970): 819–828. Note the highly original forthcoming article of Judith Modell, "Female Sexuality, Mockery, and a Challenge to Fate: A Reinterpretation of South Nayar Tālikettuka-lyānam," to appear in Sherry Ortner and Harriet Whitehead, eds., *Sexual Meanings* (forthcoming). I am grateful to Dr. Modell for having first called my attention to the Nayar and Tiyyar materials, and for having shared her excellent paper with me.

5. A. R. Radcliffe-Brown, *Structure and Function in Primitive Society* (Glencoe: Free Press, 1952), p. 37. On the details of caste organization in Malabar see Rao, 19–22; and Adrian C. Mayer, *Land and Society in Malabar* (Bombay: Oxford University Press, 1952), pp. 25–29.

6. The works of Dumont, Yalman, and Modell focus chiefly on the Nayar of South Malabar and Cochin, and the Nayar also receive more attention from Gough, "Female Initiation Rites," than any other people. Yalman's study dwells on the corresponding Sinhalese rituals, which also are the basis for Leach's article.

7. The relation of the tāli-tying rite to marriage is the main theme of most Indian discussions of the rite. See A. Aiyappan, "Meaning of the Tāli Rite," *Bulletin of the Rama Varma Research Institute* (1942); and M. D. Raghavan, "Talikettu Kalyanam," *Man in India* 9 (1929). This question is the central concern of Dumont, "Les Mariages Nayar comme faits indiens,"

and of Gough, "The Nayars and the Definition of Marriage." For a summary of the testimony before the Malabar Marriage Commission with regard to whether the tāli-tying ought to be considered a marriage in any sense, see Thurston, *Ethnographic Notes*, pp. 126ff.

8. Gough, "Tiyyar: North Kerala," p. 410.

9. Dumont, p. 35.

10. When speaking of "initiation" in India, one must be careful to differentiate two different types of ritual, both of which may be translated by this term. The first of these types is *saṃskāra,* the rituals of the life cycle, and the second is *dīkṣā,* the special consecration for one who is about to offer sacrifice or otherwise approach the sacred. In brief, the Tiyyar Tālikettu-kalyānam is primarily a *saṃskāra,* ritual, although in many ways it approximates a *dīkṣā* closely.

11. Gough, "Female Initiation Rites," pp. 48 and 57.

12. Gough, "The Nayars and the Definition of Marriage," pp. 25f.

13. The question of why there should be this insistence on initiation before puberty struck Yalman (p. 39) as one of the central analytic questions of the Tālikettukalyānam.

14. Nayar initiation as marriage has been most clearly treated by Dumont, who argues that the tāli-tying of the Nayar should be understood as a "primary" marriage, undertaken to secure proper status for woman's children, while the Nayar woman's later *sambandham* ("coupling") relations should be understood as "secondary" unions, and thus of lesser importance in ritual terms. Since the "primary" marriage is reduced to a ritual formality among the Nayar, it thus does not matter if the bride is extremely young. Comparison to child marriage elsewhere in India has been taken up briefly by Yalman, pp. 48f.

15. Gough, "Female Initiation Rites," p. 62; idem, "Tiyyar: North Kerala," p. 410; Dumont, p. 35; Yalman, p. 35.

16. The Tiyyar ceremony is most conveniently summarized in Gough, "Female Initiation Rites," pp. 57–59. Another valuable description is found in Edgar Thurston and K. Rangachari, *Castes and Tribes of Southern India,* vol. 7 (Madras: Government Press, 1909), pp. 74–81.

17. Thurston and Rangachari, p. 63, and Rao, pp. 75f, however, report that this room was to the north of the house.

18. Gough, "Female Initiation Rites," p. 57. It is not clear whether this is her own interpretation or that of informants.

19. See esp. Rao, pp. 50, 108; and Thurston and Rangachari, pp. 39f.

20. Leach, p. 822. On the role of the caste of barbers and washermen throughout South India, see Richard L. Brubaker, "Barbers, Washermen, and Other Priests: Servants of the South Indian Village and Its Goddess," *History of Religions* 19 (1979): 128–152, esp. pp. 133–135.

21. Gough, "Female Initiation Rites," p. 52.

22. Ibid, pp. 58f.

23. Gough (ibid., p. 59) foresaw this objection, and the question of the barber woman's role has since been taken up by Yalman, p. 35, and Leach, p. 822.

24. Gough, "Female Initiation Rites," pp. 49, 55, 61.

25. Thurston and Rangachari, p. 64. This rite is also reported among the Nayar of South Malabar, where it was performed by the girl's brother. Gough, "Female Initiation Rites," p. 64.

26. The term for the seat is *mana,* related to *manavalan,* "groom," and

manavati, "bride" (literally, "one who has a *mana*"). Thurston and Rangachari, p. 75.

27. Dumont, p. 35; Yalman, p. 35.

28. Although we differ on a number of specific points, Modell reaches very similar conclusions about the southern Nayar rite having the attainment of totality and androgyny as its goal.

29. This presentation, however, was apparently rejected. As Leach (pp. 824f) has shown, the gesture that immediately followed it—the girl's splitting of a coconut—symbolized the separation of the sexes, inasmuch as a coconut is thought to be androgynous until split, being then separated into male and female ends. I am inclined to see exogamy as the reason for this rejection: given the rules proscribing incest that come into marked prominence at initiation, a union of opposites based on association with one's brother would be highly improper.

30. Gough, "Female Initiation Rites," p. 63.

31. Leach, pp. 823f.

32. Rao, p. 110.

33. Note also that as early as the Indus civilization the pipal tree was often associated with male deities, but never with the goddess. E. O. James, *The Tree of Life* (Leiden: E. J. Brill, 1966), p. 21. On the margosa tree, see Gough, "Female Initiation Rites," p. 52. See also P. T. Nair, "Tree Symbol Worship among Nairs of Kerala," in Sankar Sen Gupta, ed., *Tree Symbol Worship in India* (Calcutta: Indian Publications, 1965), pp. 98–100.

34. Iyer, p. 162.

35. Thurston and Rangachari, p. 79.

36. On the cosmic tree, see Uno Holmberg (Harva), *Der Baum des Lebens* (Helsinki: Suomalainen Tiede Akatemia, 1922); also E. O. James, *The Tree of Life,* and Edric Allan Schofield Butterworth, *The Tree at the Navel of the Earth* (Berlin: De Gruyter, 1970).

37. M. S. A. Rao, *Social Change in Malabar* (Bombay: Popular Press, 1957), p. 49.

38. On Mesopotamia, see Geo Widengren, *The King and the Tree of Life in Ancient Near Eastern Religion* (Uppsala: A. B. Lundquist, 1951); on Scandinavia, Paul Bauschatz, "Urth's Well," *Journal of Indo-European Studies* 3 (1975): 53–86.

39. On child-raising, see Gough, "Tiyyar: North Kerala," p. 407. On cooking, see Rao, p. 80. On agricultural work, see Gough, "Tiyyar: North Kerala," p. 410; Rao, p. 36.

3. KINAALDÁ

1. Charlotte Johnson Frisbie, *Kinaaldá: A Study of the Navaho Girl's Puberty Ceremony* (Middletown, Conn.: Wesleyan University Press, 1967), p. 7. This book has largely superseded earlier reports of the Kinaaldá such as Edward Curtis, *The North American Indian,* vol. 1: *Apache, Jicarillas, Navaho* (Cambridge, Mass.: Harvard University Press, 1907), pp. 94–128; Gladys Reichard, *Social Life of the Navajo Indians* (New York: Columbia University Press, 1928), pp. 35–39; Leland Wyman and Flora Bailey, "Navajo Girl's Puberty Rite," *New Mexico Anthropologist* 25 (1943): 3–12; and Anne Keith, "The Navaho Girls' Puberty Ceremony," *El Palacio* 71 (1964): 27–36.

2. Gladys Reichard, *Navaho Religion: A Study of Symbolism*, 2nd ed. (Princeton: Princeton University Press, 1974), p. 173. Menarche is said to be the result of the sun's rays striking a girl in the hips (Wyman and Bailey, p. 3, n. 5).

3. Wyman and Bailey, p. 3.

4. Frisbie, p. 11. Other informants reported that the first Kinaaldá was performed "so all the people would have many babies," or "to enable her [the goddess Changing Woman, the first initiand] to create a new race and to transmit to this new race the power of generation" (Wyman and Bailey, p. 3).

5. Leland C. Wyman, *Blessingway*, recorded and translated by Father Berard Haile (Tucson: University of Arizona Press, 1970), p. 9.

6. On the various divisions, see Reichard, *Navaho Religion*, pp. 314–333; Father Berard Haile, "Navaho Chantways and Ceremonials," *American Anthropologist* 40 (1938): 639–652; Leland Wyman and Clyde Kluckhohn, "Navaho Classification of Their Song Ceremonials," *Memoirs of the American Anthropological Association* 50 (1938). On the rites in which Blessingway is used, see Wyman, pp. 3–9.

7. On the complex relation of Changing Woman, White Shell Woman, and Turquoise Woman see Reichard, *Navaho Religion*, pp. 407f, 494f; Mary C. Wheelwright, *Emergence Myth according to the Hanelthnayhe or Upward-Reaching Rite*, recorded by Father Berard Haile (Santa Fe: Museum of Navajo Ceremonial Art, 1949), pp. 132f.

8. Wyman, p. 5.

9. Frisbie, p. 9.

10. Wyman, pp. 8, 44, 50; Frisbie, p. 9.

11. Wheelwright, p. 55.

12. The summary presented here generally follows the incisive analysis of Gary Witherspoon, *Language and Art in the Navajo Universe* (Ann Arbor: University of Michigan Press, 1977). Other works on the Navajo ideology of language are: Gladys Reichard, *Prayer: The Compulsive Word* (Seattle: University of Washington Press, 1944); and Sam D. Gill, "Prayer as Person: The Performative Force in Navajo Prayer Acts," *History of Religions* 17 (1977): 143–157.

13. There is also a second set of Hogan Songs, which are used for the second Kinaaldá performed at a girl's second menstrual period. The distinction between the two sets rests on details in the myths. First Man and First Woman presided over Changing Woman's first Kinaaldá, whereas the more benevolent Talking God presided over her second, moving the ceremony to his hogan. The second set of songs are thus known as Talking God Hogan Songs, in contrast to the first set, known as Chief Hogan Songs. See Wyman, pp. 15, 169–171.

14. Frisbie, pp. 128f.

15. Ibid., p. 129.

16. Ibid., p. 357. As one informant (Dave Skeet) put it, "You tie her hair up with unwounded buckskin and let it hang down her back in a tail for four days, because that is the way *Esdzan nadle* (Changing Woman) began it" (ibid.).

17. Frisbie, p. 18.

18. Ibid., p. 350.

19. Keith, p. 27.

20. Reichard, *Social Life of the Navajo Indians*, p. 137. A few women who

are expected to bear children shortly are stroked downward, for thus the kinaaldá girl imparts an easy birth to them (Frisbie, p. 32; compare Wyman, p. 163).

21. Harold E. Driver, "Girls' Puberty Rites in Western North America," *University of California Publications in Anthropological Records* 6 (1941/42): pp. 33, 61.

22. Wyman, pp. 45.

23. Ibid., p. 163.

24. Washington Matthews, "The Night Chant," *Memoirs of the American Museum of Natural History* 6 (1902): 45, cited in Reichard, *Navaho Religion*, p. 251.

25. Flora L. Bailey, "Navaho Goods and Cooking Methods," *American Anthropologist* 42 (1940): 281. Certain details regarding the preparation of the cake have been taken from Bailey and Wyman, pp. 6–7, who offer a slightly fuller description than that of Frisbie.

26. Frisbie, p. 171.

27. Ibid., pp. 188f.

28. For the most comprehensive account of the songs and other events of the all-night sing, see Frisbie, pp. 47–59, 94–346.

29. Wyman, p. 524.

30. Frisbie, pp. 60, 354, 398; Reichard, *Social Life of the Navajo Indians*, p. 136.

31. Frisbie, p. 76.

32. Frisbie, p. 367; Wyman, p. 163.

33. Frisbie, p. 366.

34. For the specific case at hand see Katherine Spencer, *Reflections of Social Life in the Navaho Origin Myth* (Albuquerque: University of New Mexico Press, 1947), pp. 58–60. In general, on the role of ritual as repetition or reactualization of myth, see Mircea Eliade, *The Myth of the Eternal Return* (Princeton: Princeton University Press, 1954), and S. G. F. Brandon, *History, Time, and Deity* (Manchester: Manchester University Press, 1965), ch. 2.

35. Frisbie, p. 357; Reichard, *Navaho Religion*, p. 409; Wyman, p. 9.

36. Driver, p. 33.

37. Reichard, *Navaho Religion*, p. 407.

38. Wyman, p. 32. Father Berard Haile, *Origin Legend of the Navaho Enemy Way* (New Haven: Yale University Press, 1938), p. 85 and n. 11, renders her name "a woman she becomes time and again."

39. Wyman, pp. 28f.

40. Reichard, *Navaho Religion*, p. 22.

41. Wheelwright, p. 59.

42. Wyman, p. 420.

43. Haile, *Origin Legend of the Navaho Enemy Way*, p. 77.

44. Ibid., pp. 77–83.

45. Wyman, pp. 8, 44, 50; Frisbie, p. 9.

46. Wyman, p. 403.

47. Ibid., p. 509.

48. Ibid., pp. 343–348, 404f; Hasteen Klah, *Navajo Creation Myth: The Story of the Emergence*, recorded by Mary C. Wheelwright (Santa Fe: Museum of Navajo Ceremonial Art, 1942), p. 73. The deeper level of analysis is offered in Wyman, pp. 47, 141, 143.

49. Wyman, pp. 344f.

50. Frisbie, p. 11. Other versions have her growing to maturity in nine, twelve, or eighteen days, or even as long as sixteen years (Klah, p. 76).

51. Frisbie, p. 12.

52. Wyman, p. 197; Haile, *Origin Legend of the Navaho Enemy Way*, p. 93.

53. Wyman, p. 410.

54. Ibid., p. 167.

55. For the first version, see Klah, pp. 77f; for the second, Wyman, pp. 419 and 517.

56. Haile, *Origin Legend of the Navaho Enemy Way*, p. 87.

57. Ibid., p. 91; Wyman, pp. 195f.

58. Reichard, *Navaho Religion*, p. 61. In contrast to her view, I would argue that since every woman becomes Changing Woman, the sun can and ideally should have sexual relations with every woman. His promiscuity is thus a repetition of the Blessingway mythos, not a quirk of his character.

59. The first variant is presented in Haile, *Origin Legend of the Navaho Enemy Way*, p. 91; the second, in Wyman, pp. 196f, 419, and 517.

60. On the concept of *coincidentia oppositorum*, see Mircea Eliade, "Mephistopheles and the Androgyne, or the Mystery of the Whole," in *The Two and the One* (New York: Harper and Row, 1965), pp. 78–124. Other works of Eliade that have profoundly influenced my interpretations are "Mother Earth and the Cosmic Hierogamies," in *Myths, Dreams, and Mysteries* (New York: Harper and Row, 1960), pp. 155–189; and "Prolegomenon to Religious Dualism," in *The Quest* (Chicago: University of Chicago Press, 1969), pp. 127–175.

61. Klah, for instance, pp. 77f, makes no mention of water or moon. The twins are seen as the offspring of Changing Woman and Sun alone.

62. Frisbie, p. 373; Reichard, *Navaho Religion*, pp. 29, 75–77.

63. See Reichard, *Social Life of the Navajo Indians*, p. 137; Frisbie, p. 367; Wyman, p. 163.

64. The alkaan is mentioned in the following mythic accounts; Frisbie, p. 12; Haile, *Origin Legend of the Navaho Enemy Way*, p. 87; Wyman, p. 518. Klah, Wheelwright, and two out of Wyman's three informants (Slim Curley and Frank Mitchell) make no mention of the cake as having been a part of Changing Woman's Kinaaldá.

65. For the various statements, see Reichard, *Navaho Religion*, p. 266; Haile, *Origin Legend of the Navaho Enemy Way*, pp. 87 and 251, n. 16; Wyman, p. 174; Frisbie, pp. 362 and 373.

66. Reichard, *Navaho Religion*, p. 176.

67. On the obstetrical symbolism of the emergence myth, see Eliade, "Mother Earth and the Cosmic Hierogamies," pp. 155ff.

68. W. W. Hill, *The Agricultural and Hunting Methods of the Navaho Indians* (New Haven: Yale University Press, 1938), pp. 26 and 53.

69. This is similar to the way in which the participants in a Dinka sacrifice are reintegrated to the social totality, according to the analysis of Godfrey Lienhardt, *Divinity and Experience: The Religion of the Dinka* (Oxford: Clarendon Press, 1961), pp. 233f.

70. Frisbie, pp. 78, 365f.

71. Frisbie, pp. 11f, 348; Wyman, p. 9.

72. Clyde Kluckhohn and Dorothea Leighton, *The Navaho* (Garden City: Doubleday, 1962), p. 102.

73. Hill, pp. 21, 32. Note the sexual metaphor implicit in the means of

planting: the man uses a digging stick on the earth, and the women implant the seeds.

74. Kluckhohn and Leighton, p. 133.

4. TIV SCARIFICATION

1. Repairing a drum: See the Babylonian text in James B. Pritchard, ed., *Ancient Near Eastern Texts*, 3rd ed. (Princeton: Princeton University Press, 1969), pp. 334–338. Fingernails: Bruce Lincoln, "Treatment of Hair and Fingernails among the Indo-Europeans," *History of Religions* 16 (1977): 351–362.

2. On the handshake see Edmund Leach, "Ritualization in Man in Relation to Conceptual and Social Development," *Philosophical Transactions of the Royal Society*, ser. B, vol. 251 (1966): 404. On toothbrushing see Horace Miner, "Body Ritual among the Nacirema," in William Lessa and Evon Z. Vogt, eds., *Reader in Comparative Religion* (New York: Harper and Row, 1972), passim. Note also Erving Goffman, *Interaction Ritual: Essays in Face to Face Behavior* (Chicago: Aldine, 1967); Roland Barthes, *Mythologies* (London: Jonathan Cape, 1972); and Bruce Lincoln, "Two Notes on Modern Rituals," *Journal of the American Academy of Religion* 45 (1977): 147–160.

3. Rupert East, trans. and ed., *Akiga's Story: The Tiv Tribe as Seen by One of Its Members* (London: Oxford University Press, 1965), pp. 42f.

4. Ibid., 44.

5. Paul Bohannan, "Beauty and Scarification among the Tiv," *Man* 56 (1956): 118.

6. Charles F. Rowe, "Abdominal Cicatrisations of the Munshi (Tiv) Tribe, Nigeria," *Man* 28 (1928): 179.

7. Paul Bohannan, "Beauty and Scarification among the Tiv," pp. 121, 119f.

8. Ibid., p. 120.

9. Ibid.

10. Laura and Paul Bohannan, *The Tiv of Central Nigeria* (London: International African Institute, 1953), p. 65.

11. Paul Bohannan, "Circumcision among the Tiv," *Man* 54 (1954): 2, 6.

12. East, p. 32.

13. Paul Bohannan, "A Tiv Political and Religious Idea," *Southwestern Journal of Anthropology* 11 (1955): 149. What was true for the Bohannans was even more true for Abraham and Downes, the two other Western authorities on the Tiv, both of whom were British colonial officers. Even Akiga did not have access to the esoteric aspects of Tiv religion, having been converted to the Dutch Reformed Church at a very early age and having worked as a wandering preacher of the Gospel most of his life.

14. East, p. 3.

15. Laura Bohannan, "A Genealogical Charter," *Africa* 22 (1952): 301.

16. Paul Bohannan, "Concepts of Time among the Tiv of Nigeria," *Southwestern Journal of Anthropology* 9 (1953): 259.

17. The fullest treatment of Tiv uses of genealogy is that of Laura Bohannan, "A Genealogical Charter," pp. 301–315.

18. Ibid., p. 301.

19. Ibid., pp. 306f.

20. Ibid., pp. 313f.

21. Ibid., p. 301; Paul Bohannan, "A Tiv Political and Religious Idea," p. 138.

22. Paul Bohannan, "Concepts of Time among the Tiv," p. 260.

23. Paul Bohannan, "A Tiv Political and Religious Idea," pp. 138f.

24. Ibid., p. 139.

25. Ibid. (emphasis added).

26. Ibid., p. 145.

27. For treatments of the Akombo, see East, pp. 176ff; Laura and Paul Bohannan, pp. 85ff; Abraham, pp. 84ff; R. M. Downes, *The Tiv Tribe* (Kaduna: Government Printer, 1933), pp. 28 and 63; idem, *Tiv Religion* (Ibadan: Ibadan University Press, 1971), pp. 72ff. The best treatment is that of the Bohannans, which has been followed almost exclusively here.

28. With regard to the frequency with which new Akombo are adopted, note Akiga's lament that "while other peoples of the world have been advancing in knowledge of how to make all kinds of new things, progress amongst the Tiv has consisted of learning how to make more and more *Akombo*" (East, pp. 223f). Since Akiga's time, however, the use of less expensive, individually owned amulets which require no ritual practice or special knowledge on the part of the owner seems to be gaining in popularity, often at the expense of the older Akombo. See Harold M. Bergsma, "Tiv Kuraiyol, Body Protectors," *Africa* 43 (1973): 147–152.

29. On the ritual of the Akombo see Downes, *Tiv Religion*, pp. 72–78; Abraham, pp. 84ff; Laura and Paul Bohannan, pp. 87f.

30. See, for instance, Abraham, pp. 39ff; Downes, *The Tiv Tribe*, pp. 51f; idem, *Tiv Religion*, pp. 36ff; East, pp. 249ff. All these tales notwithstanding, there is not so much as one proven case of human sacrifice or cannibalism on record for the Tiv (Abraham, pp. 39, 50ff, 57).

31. East, p. 225; Laura and Paul Bohannan, p. 90; Abraham, p. 40.

32. Abraham, p. 35.

33. Ibid., p. 36.

34. On the rite of the Imborivungu, see also Downes, *The Tiv Tribe*, pp. 51f; East, pp. 227–229; Laura and Paul Bohannan, p. 90.

35. Thus Abraham, p. 42; East, p. 227.

36. East, p. 227.

37. Abraham, pp. 42f.

38. East, p. 3.

39. It is also possible that rites practiced in the past fell into disuse under the impact of British pressure. This is the opinion of Abraham, p. 58.

40. Along similar lines, although with a more one-sided social emphasis, Paul Bohannan argued that the sacrifices to repair the Imborivungu are best understood "as a metaphorical expression that the social group and its well-being must come before the life and well-being of any specific, given individual" ("A Tiv Political and Religious Idea," p. 148).

41. East, p. 228. See also Downes, *The Tiv Tribe*, p. 52, who states that all women who drink from the well will bear children, not just the first to do so.

42. Laura and Paul Bohannan, p. 90.

43. See East, pp. 296ff; Downes, *The Tiv Tribe*, pp. 12ff; and Abraham, p. 85. Note also that according to Akiga's classification, the Akombo of birth and the Akombo of the crops are one and the same (East, p. 183). The fact that the woman receives this offering on her navel rather than her hand

sets this rite apart from all those in which an Akombo is repaired after having been violated. In fact, the woman is treated like an Akombo herself, receiving the oblation, rather than as a violator who presents an offering and then receives a small portion of it back to maintain his or her new relation with the Akombo.

44. Imborivungu are depicted in Abraham, plates 2-4, 6, 7, 7B, 8B, 18, and 42; Downes, *Tiv Religion*, plates 14 and 16; and East, plate 11A. Numerous illustrations are also given in Henry Balfour, "Ritual and Secular Uses of Vibrating Membranes as Voice-Disguisers," *Journal of the Royal Anthropological Institute* 78 (1948): 45–70. Balfour maintained that Tiv Imborivungu were originally used to alter the voices of members of the Mba Tsav as they impersonated spirits or ancestors, a usage that is common among other nearby tribes but that is completely unattested for the Tiv. For refutation of his view, see Lincoln, "Religious Significance of Women's Scarification among the Tiv," pp. 317–318.

45. East, p. 43; see also Laura and Paul Bohannan, p. 66.

46. Laura and Paul Bohannan, p. 23.

47. Laura and Paul Bohannan, pp. 46f; Downes, *The Tiv Tribe*, pp. 24–26; Abraham, p. 124.

48. Paul Bohannan, "Concepts of Time among the Tiv," pp. 258f.

49. Alternatively, nongo and kwav can be seen as representing the two means whereby Tiv establish social solidarity: familial (nongo) and generational (kwav)—that is, one may feel affection for and obligation to another person either because he or she is a blood relation or a close contemporary. This interpretation in no way contradicts the one offered above, and it is possible that both are true.

50. The basic design is called the "mudfish." When "wings" are added to the design on either side of the navel, as in Figure 8, it is said to become a "swallow."

51. The Tiv interpret their history as gradual waves of expansion from a raised central point. See Akiga Sai, "The Descent of the Tiv from Ibenda Hill," trans. and ed. Paul Bohannan, *Africa* 24 (1954): 295–310, and the manuscript of Kenneth Dewar in Paul and Laura Bohannan, *A Source Notebook in Tiv History and Social Organization* (New Haven: Human Relations Area Files, 1960), pp. 1–9. On the successes of Tiv imperialism against their neighbors, see Marshall D. Sahlins, "The Segmentary Lineage: An Organization of Predatory Expansion," *American Anthropologist* 63 (1961): 322–345.

52. East, p. 43.

53. Paul Bohannan, "Beauty and Scarification among the Tiv," p. 120.

54. Laura and Paul Bohannan, pp. 16–18, 24; Abraham, p. 126. This is despite the fact that the Tiv are both patrilineal and patrilocal.

5. FESTA DAS MOÇAS NOVAS

1. This judgment is that of Alfred Métraux, "Ritos de Transito de los Indios Sudamericanos. I. La Pubertad de las Mujeres," *Anales de arqueologia y etnologia* 6 (1945): 124. The ceremony has been described numerous times; see, for example, H. Dengler, "Das Haar-Ausreissen bei den Ticuna-Indianern West-Brasiliens," *Der Erdball* 1 (1926): 231–233; Fidelis de Alviano, "Notas etnograficas sôbre os Ticunas do Alto Solimões," *Revista do Instituto*

Historico e Geografico Brasileiro 180 (1943): 15–18; and Günther Hartmann, "Festa das Moças Novas (Tukuna/Westbrasilien)," *Baessler Archiv* n.s. 15 (1967): 63–70 (based on the 1935–37 fieldwork of Siegfried Waehner). The earliest report was that of Henry Walter Bates, *The Naturalist on the River Amazons* (London: J. Murray, 1863), 2:406f. The best report to date is that of Curt Nimuendaju, *The Tukuna* (Berkeley: University of California Press, 1952), pp. 73–92; also of value is Harold Schultz, "Tukuna Maidens Come of Age," *National Geographic* 116 (1959): 628–649, with its sumptuous photographs.

2. Nimuendaju estimates that of those guests who come masked, 90 percent are men, 7 percent boys, 3 percent girls and women, although he maintains that no one is especially privileged to wear these costumes, and it is a matter of individual choice to do so (p. 80).

3. There is some memory that in the past boys were secluded when their voices broke, but this is no longer done, nor is there any memory of male circumcision, which may at one time have been practiced (Nimuendaju, pp. 40, 73).

4. Nimuendaju, pp. 8, 21, 24.

5. For the best discussion of this concern for the balance of life among a hunting and fishing people of the upper Amazon, see Gerardo Reichel-Dolmatoff, *Amazonian Cosmos: The Sexual and Religious Symbolism of the Tukuna Indians* (Chicago: University of Chicago Press, 1968), esp. pp. 50, 144f, 218f. The same general conclusion emerges from the examination of a debate some sixty-five years past. The starting point for this debate was the assertion of Hugo Kunike, "Der Fisch als Fruchtbarkeitssymbol bei den Waldindianern Südamerikas," *Anthropos* 7 (1912): 206–229, that fish figured as a general symbol of fertility throughout South America and were believed to be a powerful influence on human fertility as well. This view was quickly challenged by C. Tastevin, "Le Poisson symbole de fécondité ou de fertilité chez les Indiens de l'Amérique du Sud," *Anthropos* 9 (1914): 405–417, who, in addition to successfully disputing every major piece of evidence offered by Kunike, also astutely observed the general lack of a desire for fertility among those tribes most interested in fish and fishing (pp. 406f).

6. Nimuendaju, p. 119.

7. Ibid., p. 118.

8. Ibid., pp. 119f.

9. Ibid., p. 110.

10. Ibid.

11. See, for instance, the myth of Mo^{n}maneki's wives (Nimuendaju, pp. 151–153), or of the aicha bird who brought a drink to the twin culture heroes (ibid., p. 124). Men may also ascend to the heavens by donning feathers, as in the myth of Povaru (ibid., p. 113) and in that of the men who stole the king vulture's feathers (ibid., p. 113). Ascent by other means is also described in the myths of Orëtana (ibid., pp. 111f), Dyu^n-achiki and his daughter (ibid., p. 137), and Auëmana, the first shaman, who at death sent her soul to the sun (ibid., p. 100).

12. Nimuendaju, p. 112.

13. For legends of this happening, and fears that it will happen at any given initiation, see Nimuendaju, p. 74; Schultz, p. 640.

14. Nimuendaju, pp. 135–137.

15. Nimuendaju, p. 137. See also Alfred Métraux, *Religions et magies indiennes d'Amérique du Sud* (Paris: Gallimard, 1967), pp. 36–38; and, for more

recent movements, Mauricio Vinhas de Queiróz, " 'Cargo Cult' na Amazônia: Observações sôbre o milenarismo Tukuna," *América Latina* 6.4 (Oct.–Dec., 1963): 43–61.

16. Nimuendaju, p. 74; Hartmann, p. 64.

17. Otto Zerries, "Die Tanzmasken der Tukuna- und Juri-Taboca-Indianer," *Paideuma* 7 (1961): 374; accepted by Ute Bodiger, *Die Religion der Tukuna* (Cologne: Kölner Universitats-Verlag, 1965), p. 171. Note, however, that $pi^{n}i^{n}$ means "enclosure," as in $toki\text{-}pi^{n}i^{n}$, "the enclosure of the sacred trumpets (*toki*)," Nimuendaju, p. 76. Is it possible that $Na\text{-}pi^{n}i^{n}$ thus means "enclosure of the demons," with *na-* being an abbreviated form of *noo?*

18. Dengler, p. 232, took these innovations as signs of the degeneration of the rite.

19. Nimuendaju, p. 76.

20. Nimuendaju, p. 58; Schultz, p. 640. The assertion by Wanda Hanke, *Völkerkundliche Forschungen in Südamerika* (Braunschweig: Albert Lianbach, 1964), pp. 107f, that the drawings on the wall of the seclusion chamber are totemistic figures strikes me as without base.

21. Nimuendaju, pp. 139f. The anomalous position of maize may be due to the fact that it was introduced into South America at a relatively late date by the Arawakan wave of migration. On this, see Paul Radin, *Indians of South America* (Garden City: Doubleday, 1942), pp. 30f.

22. Nimuendaju, p. 133.

23. Ibid., p. 89. See also the metaphor adopted by Claude Lévi-Strauss, *The Raw and the Cooked* (New York: Harper and Row, 1969), pp. 159f, who sees the vorëki as being "in a state of fermentation."

24. Ibid., pp. 74f.

25. Hartmann, p. 66, states that the full moon is the proper time; Schultz, p. 632, the new moon.

26. In the puberty ceremony, the turtleshell drum is played only by members of one of the Tukuna moieties, the bamboo horns and stamping tubes by the members of the other (Nimuendaju, p. 61). The music produced when all these are played together must thus be regarded as a concert (in the sense of *concert*ed effort) in which the social divisions that normally separate the tribe are obliterated and all come together for a common purpose. A similar situation is reported and sensitively analyzed for the rites of the neighboring Cubeo by Irving Goldman, "The Structure of Ritual in the Northwest Amazon," in Robert A. Manners, ed., *Process and Pattern in Culture: Essays in Honor of Julian H. Steward* (Chicago: Aldine, 1964), pp. 111–122.

27. Nimuendaju, p. 85, states only that it is a point of honor not to stop the drumbeat once it has started, but Schultz, p. 637, notes that it is believed the Noo would harm the initiand if the drums ever fell silent.

28. Nimuendaju, p. 77. The earliest mention of these sacred instruments reports their use among the nearby Yurimagua, and comes from the journal of Padre Samuel Fritz, dated 1691: "What I unearthed was unusual in this Yurimagua village; they were celebrating a feast when, from the hut where I lay, I heard the playing of a flute which caused me such a fright that I could not suffer its sound; I ordered them to cease blowing, and inquired what it was; to which they answered that in this manner they signaled and called to Guaricana [that is, Tukuna Uaricana], who was the

Devil and who since the times of their forefathers came and attended their villages visibly . . ." (cited in Nimuendaju, p. 78).

29. Nimuendaju, pp. 77f.

30. Zerries, "Die Tanzmasken," p. 373.

31. The name "Yurupari" is apparently a Tupi word, and in the Tupian tribes he appears as a spirit of the night. The name was taken up by Christian missionaries, however, as a generic term for the devil, and was transported by them across Brazil, where it came to be identified with many various local spirits. On this, see Egon Schaden, *Ensaio etno-sociológica sôbre a mitologia heróica de algunas tribos indígenas de Brasil* (São Paulo: Universidade de São Paulo, 1946), p. 141, followed by Otto Zerries, *Wild- und Buschgeister in Südamerika* (Weisbaden: Franz Steiner, 1954), p. 331. On Bëru, see Bödiger, pp. 145f. The full set of the demons is most extensively analyzed in Zerries, "Die Tanzmasken," pp. 366–374.

32. Nimuendaju, pp. 80f.

33. Ibid., p. 81. This is the second and more elaborate of two versions he gives of this myth. Other, similar versions are given by Hartmann, p. 67, and Schultz, pp. 632–637.

34. On this whole question of hunting ritual and etiquette, see, inter alia, Otto Zerries, "Primitive South America and the West Indies," in Walter Krickeberg et al., *Pre-Columbian American Religions* (New York: Holt, Rinehart and Winston, 1968), pp. 258–275.

35. Nimuendaju, p. 69.

36. Reichel-Dolmatoff, esp. pp. 42, 55.

37. Nimuendaju, p. 83; Schultz, p. 642.

38. "Do ponto de vista da moral Cristã, espectaculo bem revoltante," Alviano, p. 18. Father Alviano (p. 14) and others, most notably Hartmann, p. 70, and Dengler, p. 232, have interpreted the Noo as personifications of sexuality, "temptations of the flesh," as they attack the pubescent girl, but this seems overly specific and a bit puritanical. Still more ill-founded is the view that Alviano (p. 15) expresses, also voiced by Roberto Cardoso de Oliveira, "Totemismo Tukuna?" in *Festgabe für Herbert Baldus* (Hanover: Münstermann, 1964), p. 238, that the masks represent totemic animals or ancestors, for which I see not the slightest justification.

39. Nimuendaju, pp. 69, 87.

40. Nimuendaju, p. 88; Schultz, p. 646.

41. See Otto Zerries, "Die Bedeutung des Federschmuckes des Südamerikanischen Schamanen und dessen Beziehung zur Vogelwelt," *Paideuma* 23 (1977): 277–324, following Micea Eliade, *Shamanism: Archaic Techniques of Ecstasy* (Princeton: Princeton University Press, 1964), esp. pp. 155f, 177.

42. Note that among the Cubeo, where all men are entitled to wear headdresses of macaw feathers, the vast majority of men do not own a full set of feathers, out of fear that too much power derived from the feathers may kill the owner. Irving Goldman, *The Cubeo* (Urbana: University of Illinois Press, 1963), pp. 153f.

43. Rafael Karsten, *The Civilization of the South American Indians* (London: Kegan Paul, Trench and Trübner, 1926), pp. 77f. Although he does note some instances of women wearing feather ornaments at initiation (pp. 85, 97), Karsten gives no examples of their wearing feather crowns or red feathers of any sort.

44. Joseph H. Greenberg, "The General Classification of Central and

South American Languages," in A. F. C. Wallace, ed., *Men and Cultures* (Philadelphia: University of Pennsylvania Press, 1960), p. 794.

45. Reichel-Dolmatoff, pp. 48, 116.

46. Bödiger, p. 31. Note also the myth of "Destructive Fire," common among the eastern and central Ge tribes, in which it is told how the sun received a fiery red feather crown from a woodpecker. Lévi-Strauss, *The Raw and the Cooked*, p. 292.

47. Nimuendaju, p. 142.

48. Schultz, p. 640. He, however, takes this to be only a protection for the girl's eyes, which are unaccustomed to direct sunlight after months of seclusion.

49. Schultz, p. 646, stating, however, that this is to protect the initiand from spirits who will harm her if she sees what transpires. Nimuendaju's report differs on this point, stating that the paternal uncle et al. pull the crown over the vorëki's eyes just before they lead her out of the seclusion chamber (p. 88).

50. Nimuendaju, p. 89; Schultz, p. 646.

51. Nimuendaju, p. 89.

52. Ibid., pp. 89f. Many interpretations of the depilation have been offered, none of them entirely satisfactory. Hartmann (pp. 68, 70) and Zerries ("Primitive South America," p. 302) see it as a symbolic death; Dengler (p. 232), as a sacrifice; Alviano (p. 16), as a public display of strength; and Karsten (p. 50), as a defense against demons. No one has mentioned the connection to the Ariana myth, which seems to me of the greatest importance.

53. Nimuendaju, esp. pp. 116ff, 144ff.

54. Lévi-Strauss, *The Raw and the Cooked*, esp. pp. 164, 334–338.

55. Nimuendaju, p. 91. The conclusion that this is done to protect against the Dyëvaë comes from a similar rite performed for infants, in which this same action is explicitly interpreted thus (ibid., p. 70).

56. Nimuendaju, p. 91.

57. Ibid.

58. Ibid.

59. Ibid., p. 92.

60. Ibid., pp. 21, 24. Note also the analysis of Lévi-Strauss, *The Raw and the Cooked*, pp. 267–278, who assesses timbó first as a means of procuring food that is not itself food, thus "an inedible food" (p. 267), and second as a natural substance that streamlines or makes more efficient the cultural process of fishing, thus "an intrusion of nature into culture" (p. 276).

61. Reichel-Dolmatoff, p. 229.

62. Nimuendaju, p. 93. The associations to marriage are so strong that when Bates first saw the rite performed during his voyage of 1857–58, he took it to be a wedding celebration (Nimuendaju, p. 10).

63. Nimuendaju, p. 93.

6. THE RAPE OF PERSEPHONE

1. Vedic India: Reconstructions are possible, for instance, on the basis of the Brahmānas and Śrauta Sūtras. See, inter alia, P.-E. Dumont, *L'Agnihotra: Description de l'agnihotra dans le rituel védique* (Baltimore: Johns Hopkins

University Press, 1939), and J. C. Heestermann, *The Ancient Indian Royal Consecration* (The Hague: Mouton, 1957). A selection of ritual texts from the ancient Near East may be found in James B. Pritchard, ed., *Ancient Near Eastern Texts*, 3rd ed. (Princeton: Princeton University Press, 1969), pp. 325–361. On the basis of such texts have come such reconstructions as Samuel Noah Kramer, *The Sacred Marriage Rite* (Bloomington: Indiana University Press, 1969), and Heinrich Otten, *Hethitische Totenrituale* (Berlin: Akademie Verlag, 1958).

Peoples of Europe: See, for instance, Johannes Maringer, *The Gods of Prehistoric Man* (London: Weidenfeld and Nicolson, 1960), esp. pp. 34–37, 40–43, 100–105; Marija Gimbutas, *The Gods and Goddesses of Old Europe* (Berkeley: Univerity of California Press, 1974), esp. pp. 57–66, 72–85.

Folk dances and customs: For instance, Marcel Granet, *Danses et légendes de la chine ancienne*, 2 vols. (Paris: F. Alcan, 1926); E. Gasparini, "La danza circolare degli slavi," *Ricerche Slavistiche* 3 (1954): 72–89; E. C. Cawte, *Ritual Animal Disguise* (Totowa, N.J.: Rowman & Littlefield, 1978).

2. See, for example, Lily Weiser, *Altgermanische Jünglingsweihe und Männerbünde* (Baden: Konkordia A.-G., 1927); Richard Wolfram, "Sword Dances and Secret Societies," *Journal of the English Folk Dance and Song Society* 1 (1932): 34–41; Otto Höfler, *Kultische Geheimbünde der Germanen* (Frankfurt: Moritz Diesterweg, 1934); Stig Wikander, *Der arische Männerbund* (Lund: Gleerupska Universitets Bokhandeln, 1938); Gerhard Binder, *Die Aussetzung des Königskindes Kyros und Romulus* (Meisenheim: Anton Hain, 1964); Geo Widengren, "Le Symbolisme de la ceinture," *Iranica Antiqua* 8 (1968): 133–155. For the preservation of a scenario of women's initiation in a well-known fairy tale, see N. J. Girardot, "Initiation and Meaning in the Tale of Snow White and the Seven Dwarfs," *Journal of American Folklore* 90 (1977): 274–300.

3. On the Romans, see especially J. Gagé, *Matronalia* (Brussels: Collection Latomus, 1963). Arrephoria: Walter Burkert, "Kekropidensage und Arrephoria: Vom Initiationsritus zum Panathenäenfest," *Hermes* 94 (1966): 1–25. Brauronia: Angelo Brelich, *Paides e Parthenoi*, vol. 1 (Rome: Ateneo, (1969), esp. pp. 240–279. A brief English summary of his views is available in Angelo Brelich, "Symbol of a Symbol," in J. M. Kitagawa and C. H. Long, eds., *Myths and Symbols: Studies in Honor of Mirecea Eliade* (Chicago: University of Chicago Press, 1969), pp. 201–206. Thesmophoria: J. Prytz Johansen, "The Thesmophoria as a Women's Festival," *Temenos* 11 (1975): 78–87. Haloa: G. E. Skov, "The Priestess of Demeter and Kore and Her Role in the Initiation of Women at the Festival of the Haloa at Eleusis," *Temenos* 11 (1975): 136–147.

4. As an allegory of the seasons by L. Preller, *Griechische Mythologie,* 4th ed., revised by Carl Robert (Berlin: Weidmann, 1894), p. 765–769; Jane Ellen Harrison, *Prolegomena to the Study of Greek Religion* (Cambridge: Cambridge University Press, 1903), pp. 271–276; Lewis Richard Farnell, *Cults of the Greek States* (Oxford: Clarendon Press, 1907), 3:114; James George Frazer, *Spirits of the Corn and Wild*, vol. 1, in *The Golden Bough*, 3rd ed., pt. 5 (London: Macmillan, 1912), pp. 35–91, esp. pp. 35 and 78; Harold R. Willoughby, *Pagan Regeneration* (Chicago: University of Chicago Press, 1929), p. 42; Ulrich von Wilamowitz-Moellendorff, *Der Glaube der Hellenen* (Berlin: Weidmann, 1932), 2:51f; and Vilhelm Gronbech, *Götter und Menschen: Griechische Geistesgeschichte* (Hamburg: Rowohlt, 1967), pp. 195ff.

As an allegory of the grain by F. M. Cornford, "The *Aparkhai* and the

Eleusinian Mysteries," in *Essays and Studies Presented to William Ridgeway* (Cambridge: Cambridge University Press, 1913), pp. 153–166; M. P. Nilsson, "Die eleusinischen Gottheiten," *Archiv für Religionswissenschaft* 32 (1935): 79–141, esp. pp. 101–119; idem, *Greek Folk Religion* (New York: Harper and Row, 1961), pp. 42–64.

As a scenario of women's initiation by H. Jeanmaire, *Couroi et Courètes* (Lille: Bibliothèque Universitaire, 1939), pp. 269–279, 298–305. Similar ideas had already been presented by Otto Kern, *Die griechischen Mysterien der Klassischen Zeit* (Berlin: Weidmann, 1927), p. 25; Felix Speiser, "Die Eleusinischen Mysterien als primitive Initiation," *Zeitschrift für Ethnologie* 60 (1928): 362–372; and Wilamowitz-Moellendorff, 2:52f.

5. For instance, Walter Burkert did not even mention Jeanmaire's thesis in his treatment of Eleusis in *Homo Necans* (Berlin: W. de Gruyter, 1972), pp. 274–327, or in *Griechische Religion der archaischen und klassischen Epoche* (Stuttgart: W. Kohlhammer, 1977), pp. 247–251. Neither does F. Graf in *Eleusis und die orphische Dichtung Athens in vorhellenistischer Zeit* (Berlin: W. de Gruyter, 1974). N. J. Richardson, *The Homeric Hymn to Demeter* (Oxford: Clarendon Press, 1964), p. 17, dismisses Jeanmaire quite abruptly.

6. See Marija Gimbutas, *The Gods and Goddesses of Old Europe* (Berkeley: University of California Press, 1974); "The First Wave of Eurasian Steppe Pastoralists into Copper Age Europe," *Journal of Indo-European Studies* 5 (1977): 277–338, esp. p. 281.

7. Angelo Brelich, "The Historical Development of the Institution of Initiation in the Classical Ages," *Acta Antiqua* 9 (1961): 267–283.

8. According to Pausanias 1.38.3, a historic conflict between the cities of Athens and Eleusis (which are very close to one another) was resolved by leaving the administration of the Mysteries to Eleusis, with all governmental, economic, and military matters passing to Athenian control.

9. His etymology and interpretation are now accepted by most standard sources, such as Hjalmar Frisk, *Griechisches etymologisches Wörterbuch* (Heidelberg: Carl Winter, 1973), 1:920f; and Julius Pokorny, *Indogermanisches etymologisches Wörterbuch* (Bern: Francke, 1959), p. 577. A similar interpretation, without supporting etymological evidence, had already been presented by Victor Magnien, "Le Mariage chez les grecs," *Mélanges Franz Cumont* (Brussels: Institut d'Histoire et de Philologie Orientales et Slaves, 1934), pp. 318f.

10. As in Pausanias 3.16.1, noted by Brelich, *Paides e Parthenoi*, p. 162, n. 145. Note also Sophokles, Fragment 804, in S. Radt, *Tragicorum Graecorum Fragmenta*, vol. 4 (Göttingen: Vandenhoeck and Ruprecht, 1977), p. 543, and the lines of Karkinos preserved in Diodoros Sikulos 5.5.1, where Kore is called *parthenos*.

11. Claudian, *De Raptu Proserpinae*, 1.131; Ovid, *Fasti*, 4.417; Arnobius of Sicca, *Adversus Nationes*, 5.24. Ovid, *Metamorphoses* 5.376f, states that it was the fear that Proserpine might remain virgin that motivated Pluto to rape her.

12. Claudian, *De Raptu Proserpinae*, 1.133–137; Nonnos, *Dionysiaka*, 6.1–3; Firmicus Maternus, 7.1.

13. L. Gernet and A. Boulanger, *Le Génie grec dans la religion* (Paris: La Renaissance du Livre, 1932), pp. 39f, cited by Paolo Scarpi, *Letture sulla Religione Classica: L'Inno Omerico a Demetra* (Florence: Leo Olschke, 1976), pp. 109f.

14. All translations are original. The text used is that of N. J. Rich-

ardson, *The Homeric Hymn to Demeter* (Oxford: Clarendon Press, 1964), with its copious and extremely helpful annotation.

15. See also Hesiod, *Theogony*, 914; Apollodoros, *Bibliotheka*, 1.5.1; Diodoros Sikelos, 5.68.2; Isokrates, *Panegyrikos*, 28; Orphic Fragment 49, l. 37, in Otto Kern, *Orphicorum Fragmenta*, 2nd ed. (Berlin: Weidmann, 1965), p. 120. Clement of Alexandria, *Protreptikos*, 2.14; Nonnos, *Dionysiaka*, 6.92.

16. Claudian, *De Raptu Proserpina*, 1.27, title et passim; Ovid, *Fasti*, 4.417; *Metamorphoses*, 5.395.

17. The significance of this painting was first recognized by Karl Kerenyi, "Persephone und Prometheus vom alter griechischer Mythen," K. Hoppe, ed., *Hans Oppermann Festschrift*, in *Jahrbuch der Raabe Gesellschaft* (1965), pp. 58–61.

18. Text in J. B. Hall, ed., *Claudian: De Raptu Proserpinae* (Cambridge: Cambridge University Press, 1969), p. 51.

19. *De Raptu Proserpinae*, 2.226–231. See also Orphic Fragment 49, ll. 41–45; Clement of Alexandria, *Protreptikos*, 2.14.

20. Text from M. L. West, *Hesiod: Theogony* (Oxford: Clarendon Press, 1966), p. 145.

21. See, for instance, Ugo Bianchi, "Sagezza olimpica e mistica eleusina nell'Inno Omerico a Demetra," *Studi e Materiali di Storia delle Religioni* 35 (1964): 166–168, 176–180.

22. H. Phelps Gates, *The Kinship Terminology of Homeric Greek* (Bloomington: Indiana University Press, 1971), pp. 5–8.

23. Most recently, Scarpi, pp. 109–138. Scarpi's point is not, however, that the myth served as an etiology for marriage customs, but rather—in keeping with his fascinating and highly original structuralist interpretation of the myth—that as a bride Persephone mediates between Olympos and the underworld. For an equally interesting but somewhat less successful structuralist analysis of the myth, see William Berg, "Eleusinian and Mediterranean Harvest Myths," *Fabula* 15 (1974): 202–211.

24. Walter Erdmann, *Die Ehe im alten Griechenland* (Munich: C. H. Beck, 1934), pp. 179f. Scarpi, attempting to salvage his thesis, argues first that the gods are not bound to observe human exogamic marriage laws (pp. 117ff), and, second, misinterpreting the argument of Jean Vernant, "Le Mariage en Grèce archaïque," *La parola del passato* 148 (1973): 66f, that marriage to the mother's brother did occur in some upper-class Greek families (p. 125n). Even if this were the case, one cannot escape the fact that Hades is also Persephone's father's brother, to whom marriage would be quite impossible in any event. On balance, I am thus inclined to reject any view of the abduction as a marriage rite.

25. As stressed by Nilsson, "Die eleusinischen Gottheiten," pp. 105–107; and Walter Otto, "The Meaning of the Eleusinian Mysteries," in Joseph Campbell, ed., *Papers from the Eranos Yearbooks*, vol. 2: *The Mysteries* (Princeton: Princeton University Press, 1955), pp. 17f.

26. For the use of the term "underworld" in an initiatory context, see: Mircea Eliade, *Rites and Symbols of Initiation* (New York: Harper and Row, 1958), pp. 13f, 61–64, 132; Arnold van Gennep, *The Rites of Passage* (Chicago: University of Chicago Press, 1960), pp. 75 and 81; W. F. Jackson Knight, *Cumaean Gates* (Oxford: Basil Blackwell, 1936), esp. pp. 3–7.

27. On this and other aspects of the so-called liminal state, see Victor Turner, "Betwixt and Between: The Liminal Period in *Rites de Passage*," in *The Forest of Symbols* (Ithaca: Cornell University Press, 1967), pp. 93–102.

28. Literally, *parakoitis* denotes "he or she who lies beside one in bed." Hesychius glosses the term as *pallakis*, "concubine," and Diodoros Sikelos 5.32.7, understands it in the same way, as has been noted by Scarpi, p. 121. The *Homeric Hymn* is totally—and no doubt consciously—devoid of all the normal Greek terminology directly relevant to marriage: *gameō*, "to marry;" *gynē*, "wife;" *nymphos*, "bridegroom," and so on—a fact reluctantly noted by Scarpi, p. 120.

29. See, for instance, the stories of Helen and Theseus, Boreas and Oreithya, the Dioskuroi and the daughters of Leukippos, the rape of the Athenian women by the Pelasgians at the Brauronia festival, and that of the Spartan virgins at the Hyakinthia, all of which have been treated as evidence of archaic Greek rites of female initiation, by Brelich, *Paides e Parthenoi*, pp. 138, 146, 162n, 163n, 165, 241, 246, 277f, 283f.

30. J. S. La Fontaine, "Ritualization of Women's Life-Crises in Bugisu," in J. S. La Fontaine, ed., *The Interpretation of Ritual: Essays in Honour of A. I. Richards* (London: Tavistock, 1972), pp. 167f.

31. W. K. C. Guthrie, *The Greeks and Their Gods* (Boston: Beacon Press, 1950), p. 284.

32. Günther Zuntz, *Persephone* (Oxford: Clarendon Press, 1971), pp. 73–77; Nilsson, *Greek Folk Religion*, p. 53.

33. Thus, V. Puntoni, *L'Inno Omerico a Demetra* (Livorno: R. Giusti, 1896), esp. pp. 5, 8; Richardson, pp. 81, 155f; Wilamowitz, 2:51; Franz Bücheler, *Berliner Klassikertexte*, vol. 5.1 (Berlin: Weidmann, 1907), pp. 16–18; L. Malten, "Altorphische Demetersagen," *Archiv für Religionswissenschaft* 12 (1909): 418; T. Kraus, *Hekate* (Heidelberg: Carl Winter, 1960), pp. 63f; and Robert Böhme, *Orpheus: Der Sänger und seine Zeit* (Bern: Francke, 1970), p. 108. The role of Hekate in the *Homeric Hymn* is very curious. She makes two brief apperances, both of which are suspicious. In the first (ll. 51–58), despite the testimony of ll. 22–23 that "not one of the immortals . . . heard her voice," Hekate is said to have heard Kore's cries, and on the basis of this she tells Demeter that her daughter has been abducted. On no other incident in the entire myth is there so much disagreement in the sources as on the question of Demeter's informants. The "Orphic" sources state that it was the inhabitants of Eleusis who revealed Kore's whereabouts; Ovid, that it was the nymph Cyane; Pausanias, that it was Khrysanthis; Apollodoros, that it was the people of Hermion; and Firmicis Maternus, that it was Pandarus. There is no reason to assume that the testimony of the *Homeric Hymn* is either authoritative or very old on this point. The second appearance of Hekate (ll. 438–440) is even more suspect. Here, Hekate makes an extremely brief appearance between two long and crucial scenes of the hymn: the reunion of Demeter and Persephone (ll. 384–437), and the mission of Rheia from Zeus to Demeter, urging their reconciliation (ll. 441–469). The scene with Hekate adds nothing to the narrative, and seems to have been inserted here for no intrinsically compelling reason. Furthermore, when Hekate speaks, she addresses Persephone as *korē*, using the Attic form of the word, whereas in every other occurrence in the *Hymn* the Homeric form *kourē* is used. This piece of linguistic evidence clearly indicates an Athenian redaction whereby Hekate has been introduced into the text, no doubt in order to justify her role in the Eleusinian cult.

34. Van Gennep, esp. p. 77; Eliade, *Rites and Symbols of Initiation*, pp. 28, 31, 68, 74f.

35. On Baubo and Iambe, see Albrecht Dieterich, *Eine Mithrasliturgie*

(Leipzig: B. G. Teubner, 1903), pp. 123–126; Charles Picard, "L'Episode de Baubo dans les Mystères d'Eleusis," *Revue de l'histoire des religions* 95 (1927): 220–255; and Isidore Levy, "Autour d'un roman mythologique égyptien," in *Mélanges Franz Cumont*, pp. 819–834; all of which are extremely suggestive, but none fully convincing.

36. Text in G. W. Butterworth, *Clement of Alexandria* (New York: G. P. Putnam, 1919), pp. 42f. *Hypo kolpois* is probably a euphemism for "into the vagina" rather than for "beneath the breasts," the more literal translation, and this is more fitting with the verb (*riptaskō*). The action thus described would be a ritual mimicry of sexual intercourse, something quite appropriate to the Eleusinian rites and to women's initiations in general.

37. See Eliade, *Rites and Symbols of Initiation*, p. 45; idem, *Myths, Dreams and Mysteries* (New York: Harper and Row, 1960), pp. 212ff; and Richard Wolfram, "Weiberbünde," *Zeitschrift für Volkskunde* 42 (1932): 137–142.

38. See, for instance, Nilsson, *Greek Folk Religion*, p. 50.

39. The importance of this episode has been recognized by Jeanmaire, pp. 298ff, 304f; and Mircea Eliade, *Histoire des croyances et des idées religieuses* (Paris: Payot, 1976), 1:304f.

40. The plunging of the world into a state of *akosmia*, "cosmic disorder," literally "non-cosmos," as a major theme in the *Homeric Hymn* has been ably developed by Scarpi, esp. p. 73.

41. Thus Isokrates, *Panegyrikos*, 28; Ovid, *Fasti*, 4.401f, 509; Kallimakhos, Hymn 6, ll. 18–21; Diodoros Sikelos 5.68.2; Pausanias, 1.14.2f; Claudian, *De Raptu Proserpinae*, 1.30f. On the use of the mission of Triptolemos as a theme in art, see Mylonas, pp. 193, 195–197.

42. On the myth as relating the transformation of man from food-gatherer to food-producer, see the extremely interesting work of Ileana Chirassi, *Elementi di culture precereali nei miti e riti greci* (Rome: Ateneo, 1968), pp. 75f, 88f, 190f; G. Piccaluga, "Ta Pherephattēs Anthologia," *Maia* 18 (1966): 232–253; and Scarpi, pp. 42–72, 89–95.

43. *Homeric Hymn*, ll. 396–403. Some sources specify that she will spend half her year in the underworld and half on Olympos, and others tell that she ate three or seven, rather than just one seed.

44. Kerenyi, *Eleusis*, pp. 137ff.

45. See Chirassi, pp. 73–90; Uberto Pestalozza, *L'Eternel féminin dans la religion méditerranéenne* (Brussels: Collection Latomus, 1965), p. 53; and Eugene S. McCartney, "How the Apple Became the Token of Love," *Transactions of the American Philological Association* 56 (1925): 78f, on the symbolism of the pomegranate.

46. A. Carnoy, *Dictionnaire etymologique des noms grecs des plantes* (Louvain: Publications Universitaire, 1959), pp. 87f, noted by Scarpi, p. 98n.

47. George Mylonas, *Eleusis and the Eleusinian Mysteries* (Princeton: Princeton University Press, 1961), p. 281.

48. For the most recent detailed attempts to reconstruct what happened at Eleusis, see the extremely cautious, sober work of Mylonas, and the exuberant, highly speculative book of Kerenyi, esp. pp. 5–102.

49. Regarding dress, it was not until A.D. 166–169 that white clothing was introduced, according to Philostratos, *Lives of the Sophists* 2.1. On the route traveled, see Richardson, p. 189. On the use of torches, see Clement of Alexandria, *Protreptikos*, 2.12; Lactantius, *Epitome Institutionum Divinarum*, 23.7; Statius Silvius, 4.8.50f.

50. Strabo, 9.400; Hesykhios, under *gephyris-gephyristai*.

51. The synthema goes on to describe certain ritual manipulations of objects contained in baskets, on which there has been considerable scholarly debate. The recent trend, however, as evidenced in Mylonas, p. 301, and Nilsson, *Greek Popular Religion*, p. 45, is to accept only fasting and drinking the *kykeon* as legitimate parts of the Eleusinian rites. Kerenyi, *Eleusis*, pp. 177–180, and "Voraussetzungen der Einweihung in Eleusis," in C. J. Bleecker, ed., *Initiation* (Leiden: E. J. Brill, 1965), pp. 62f, has argued that the contents of the *kykeon* as described in the *Homeric Hymn* could aid the Mystai to a visionary experience if it was drunk after a period of fasting.

52. See Richardson, p. 201.

53. Kerenyi, *Eleusis*, pp. 80f.

54. Thus, the hierophant, chief priest of the Mysteries, was always drawn from the family of the Eumolpidae, descendants of the Eleusinian hero Eumolpus, mentioned in 1.475 of the *Homeric Hymn*. See Richardson, pp. 183, 197f.

55. Mylonas, p. 282.

56. Kerenyi, *Eleusis*, p. 24.

57. Ibid., p. 90.

58. This has been convincingly shown by Kerenyi, *Eleusis*, pp. 88ff, on which point his account is preferable to that of Mylonas.

59. Tertullian, *Against the Valentinians*, 1; Hippolytos, *Philosophoumena*, 5.8.38–41.

60. Text in Achille Vogliano, ed., *Papiri dell' Università degli Studi di Milano*, vol. 1 (Milan: Ulrico Hoepli, 1937), pp. 176f.

61. The importance of this text was first recognized by Otto, p. 27. His argument has been supported by Kerenyi, *Eleusis*, pp. 83f; and Eliade, *Histoire des croyances et des idées religieuses*, 1:312.

62. Text in C. Wendel, *Scholia in Theocritum Vetera* (Stuttgart: B. G. Teubner, 1967), p. 279.

63. Otto, p. 27. See also Kerenyi, *Eleusis*, pp. 84, 94.

64. Numerous texts claim that participation in the Mysteries would win one a blessed afterlife. See the *Homeric Hymn to Demeter*, ll. 480–482; Sophokles, Fragment 837, in Radt, p. 553; and Pindar, Fragment 137, in Bruno Snell, ed., *Pindarus* (Leipzig: B. G. Teubner, 1964), 2:112.

65. On the date of the temple complex at Eleusis, see Mylonas, pp. 14, 33. For earlier evidence of the Persephone myth, Kerenyi, "Persephone und Prometheus: Vom alter griechischer Mythen;" and for evidence of the goddess, albeit in somewhat different form, as early as the third millennium B.C., Zuntz, esp. pp. 7–13.

66. Brelich, *Paides e Parthenoi*, pp. 237, 289–297, 311; Burkert, pp. 19f.

7. ON THE NATURE OF WOMEN'S INITIATIONS

1. See Judith K. Brown, "A Cross-Cultural Study of Female Initiation Rites," *American Anthropologist* 65 (1963): 837–853; contested by Harold E. Driver, "Girls' Puberty Rites and Matrilocal Residence," *American Anthropologist* 71 (1969): 905–908.

2. The Tukuna offer one example of this. For women's initiations practiced by hunters, see: George Bird Grinnell, *The Cheyenne Indians* (rpt. Lin-

coln: University of Nebraska Press, 1972), 1:129f; Josef Haekel, "Jugend-weihe und Männerfest auf Feuerland," *Mitteilungen der Österreichischen Gesellschaft für Anthropologie* 73–77 (1947): 102f, and Roland M. and Catherine H. Berndt, *The World of the First Australians* (Chicago: University of Chicago Press, 1964), pp. 150–157. For those practiced by fishers: Peter Kloos, "Female Initiation among the Maroni River Caribs," *American Anthropologist* 71 (1969): 898–905; Niels Fock, *Waiwai: Religion and Society of an Amazonian Tribe* (Copenhagen: National Museum, 1963), pp. 154–157; and A. R. Radcliffe-Brown, *The Andaman Islanders* (Glencoe: Free Press, 1964), pp. 92ff. For those practiced by pastoralists: Peter Rigby, "The Structural Context of Girls' Puberty Rites," *Man* 2 (1967): 434–444; John G. Kennedy, "Circumcision and Excision in Egyptian Nubia," *Man* 5 (1970): 175–191; and Ronald A. Reminick, "The Symbolic Significance of Ceremonial Defloration among the Amhara of Ethiopia," *American Ethnologist* 3 (1976): 751–763. Modern urban commercial society, for its part, is replete with rituals of women's initiation—graduations, confirmations, first dates, and weddings, to name a few.

3. On the position of women in ancient Greece, see Walter Erdmann, *Die Ehe im alten Griechenland*, pp. 1–86; Johannes Leipoldt, *Die Frau in der antiken Welt und im Urchristentums* (Gütersloh: Gerd Mohn, 1962), pp. 18–49; and Moses I. Finley, *The World of Odysseus* (New York: Viking, 1965), pp. 136–140.

4. Aristotle, *Physics,* bk. 2, sect. 3 (194b).

5. It is, of course, possible that there will be a set of agents, as, for instance, where women initiate women but do so at the behest of men. In such instances, it is the original or prime agents who are of interest for our analysis, not the intermediate agents.

6. This, it strikes me, is a quasi-pornographic model of initiation, reminiscent of the works of the Marquis de Sade and *The Story of O.* In a certain sense these can be considered examples of women's initiation, existing at the extreme end of the spectrum of cruelty involved and that of male domination of the culture in which such rites are practiced, given that the cultural context is the imagination of their authors.

7. It is entirely possible for a Navajo woman to act as chief singer, although this is not the usual state of affairs.

8. Nimeundaju, *The Tukuna,* p. 88.

9. Ibid., p. 90.

10. Max Gluckman, "Les Rites de Passage," in Max Gluckman, ed., *Essays on the Ritual of Social Relations* (Manchester: Manchester University Press, 1962), p. 40. See also pp. 39–41, 46f.

11. Frisbie, *Kinaaldá,* p. 359.

12. Ibid.

13. Ibid., p. 381. On the notion of "beauty," see also Gary Witherspoon, *Language and Art in the Navajo Universe* (Ann Arbor: University of Michigan Press, 1977), esp. pp. 150–154.

14. Following the well-known theories of myth and time advanced by Mircea Eliade, which have been most influential on my analysis, here and elsewhere. For the most convenient summary, see *The Sacred and the Profane* (New York: Harcourt, Brace, 1959), pp. 68–113.

15. Harold E. Driver, "Girls' Puberty Rites in Western North America," *University of California Publications in Anthropological Records* 6 (1941): 33.

16. These are only a few of the terms the Navajo use to denote corn at

various stages of its development and usage. According to W. W. Hill, *The Agricultural and Hunting Methods of the Navaho Indians* (New Haven: Yale University Press, 1938), p. 33, more than twenty different stages are recognized and named. One might also argue, in the manner of Lévi-Strauss, that it is the act of cooking that mediates between or synthesizes corn batter and corn cake. It is interesting, however, that both these alternative interpretations point to phenomena that are closely associated with adult female status among the Navajo: cooking and agriculture.

17. Van Gennep, *Rites of Passage*, p. 3.

18. Ibid., p. 10.

19. On the ambiguity of the liminal state, see van Gennep, *Rites of Passage*, pp. 26, 82, 114f. In addition, see the probing treatment of Victor Turner, "Betwixt and Between: The Liminal Period in *Rites de Passage*," in *The Forest of Symbols* (Ithaca: Cornell University Press, 1967), pp. 93–102.

20. Van Gennep, *Rites of Passage*, pp. 15–25.

21. Ibid., p. 192.

22. Van Gennep's chapter on initiation (pp. 65–115) falls into three sections: tribal initiations (pp. 74–88), initiation into the international, soteriologically oriented religions (pp. 88–100), and initiation into castes, classes, and professions (pp. 101–113). The latter two of these categories are not really defined in sex-specific terms. Of the twenty-five tribal initiations that are discussed at any length, nineteen are exclusively male (Lillooet, Hottentot, Elema, various groups in Morocco, Senegal and Australia, Kwakiutl, Omaha, Ojibway, Zuni, Yaunde, secret societies of the Congo, Guinea, and Melanesia, Fiji, Arioi, Banks Islands, Oba, and Arapaho); four involve both sexes (Thomson Indians, Navajo, Mandaeans, and Masai); and only two are rites of women's initiation proper (Toda and Yao). (These assessments are based on the material as van Gennep presents it. In some instances, ethnographic investigation since his time would alter the picture, as, for instance, research into the women's secret societies of Guinea.)

23. Van Gennep, *The Rites of Passage*, p. 192.

24. Above all, see Simone de Beauvoir, *The Second Sex*, tr. H. M. Parshley (New York: Bantam Books, 1961). An extremely interesting article that combines feminist and anthropological perspectives is Sherry Ortner, "Is Female to Male as Nature Is to Culture?" in Michelle Rosaldo and Louise Lamphere, eds., *Woman, Culture, and Society* (Stanford: Stanford University Press, 1974), pp. 67–87. In contrast, see the thoroughly embarrassing and occasionally insulting essay of E. E. Evans-Pritchard, "The Position of Women in Primitive Societies and in Our Own," in *The Position of Women in Primitive Societies and Other Essays* (Oxford: Clarendon Press, 1966).

25. Meyer Fortes, "Ritual and Office in Tribal Society," in Gluckman, ed., *Essays on the Ritual of Social Relations*, pp. 52ff.

26. Van Gennep, *Rites of Passage*, p. 67; Fortes, p. 87.

27. Van Gennep, *Rites of Passage*, p. 67.

28. Turner, *The Ritual Process*, pp. 94–130.

29. Ibid., p. 95.

30. Ibid.

31. Ibid., p. 96.

32. Ibid., p. 126.

33. This may explain the solidarity of extremely oppressed women such as the Mundurucu, who seem to lie in a permanent state of communitas as

they are described by Robert and Yolanda Murphy, *Women of the Forest* (New York: Columbia University Press, 1974).

34. Turner, *The Ritual Process,* p. 95.

35. This is perhaps a bit of an overstatement. Nudity does occur occasionally, although with far less frequency than in male rites and with quite different significance. Thus, for instance, the Tiyyar woman bathes before she is dressed for her Tālikettukalyānam, and is naked for her bath. This is observed by no one, however, and is an incidental part of purificatory preparations for the ritual. It does not serve to reduce the initiand to nothingness.

36. Charles Keil, *Tiv Song* (Chicago: University of Chicago Press, 1979), p. 223.

37. This is not to say that men's initiations never confer a cosmic status: occasionally they do, particularly in the initiation rites for such exalted individuals as kings, priests, shamans, and the like, but these are a special case. In the more general initiations that grant adult male status only, a cosmic component is less likely to be present, and when present it tends to play a subordinate role to concern with sociopolitical status.

38. For Bachofen's theories, see J. J. Bachofen, *Das Mutterrecht,* ed. Karl Meuli, 2 vols. (Basel: B. Schwabe, 1948). These theories, long abandoned by most scholars, have now been administered the *coup de grace* by Joan Bamberger, "The Myth of Matriarchy," in Rosaldo and Lamphere, eds., *Woman, Culture, and Society,* pp. 263–280.

39. Keith, p. 30. Ellipsis in original.

40. Ibid., p. 33. Italics added.

41. Ibid., pp. 32. See also p. 35.

42. Ibid., p. 33.

Bibliography

Abraham, R. C. *The Tiv People*. 2nd ed. London: Crown Agents for the Colonies, on behalf of the Government of Nigeria, 1940.

Akiga Sai. "The Descent of the Tiv from Ibenda Hill," tr. and ed. Paul Bohannan. *Africa* 24 (1954): 295–310.

Allen, M. R. *Male Cults and Secret Initiations in Melanesia*. Melbourne: Melbourne University Press, 1967.

Alviano, Fidelis de. "Notas etnograficas sóbre os Ticunas do Alto Solimões." *Revista do Instituto Historico e Geografico Brasileiro* 180 (1943): 5–34.

d'Alviella, Goblet. "L'Initiation: Institution sociale, magique et religieuse." *Revue de l' Histoire des Religions* 81 (1920): 1–28.

Bachofen, J. J. *Das Mutterrecht*, ed. Karl Meuli. 2 vols. Basel: B. Schwabe, 1948.

Bailey, Flora L. "Navaho Foods and Cooking Methods." *American Anthropologist* 42 (1940): 270–290.

Balfour, Henry. "Ritual and Secular Uses of Vibrating Membranes as Voice-Disguisers." *Journal of the Royal Anthropological Institute* 78 (1948): 45–70.

Bamberger, Joan. "The Myth of Matriarchy." In Michelle Rosaldo and Louise Lamphere, eds., *Woman, Culture, and Society*. Stanford: Stanford University Press, 1974, pp. 263–280.

Barthes, Roland. *Mythologies*. London: Jonathan Cape, 1972.

Bates, Henry Walter. *The Naturalist on the River Amazons*. 2 vols. London: J. Murray. 1863.

Bauschatz, Paul. "Urth's Well." *Journal of Indo-European Studies* 3 (1975): 53–86.

Beauvoir, Simone de. *The Second Sex*. New York: Bantam Books, 1961.

Berg, William. "Eleusinian and Mediterranean Harvest Myths," *Fabula* 15 (1974): 202–211.

Bergsma, Harold M. "Tiv *Kuraiyol*, Body Protectors." *Africa* 43 (1973): 147–152.

Berndt, Roland M. and Catherine H. *The World of the First Australians*. Chicago: University of Chicago Press, 1964.

Bettelheim, Bruno. *Symbolic Wounds: Puberty Rites and the Envious Male*. New York: Collier, 1962.

Bianchi, Ugo. "Sagezza olimpico e mistica eleusina nell' Inno Omerico a Demetra." *Studi e Materiali di Storia delle Religioni* 35 (1964): 161–194.

Binder, Gerhard. *Die Aussetzung des Königskindes Kyros und Romulus*. Meisenheim: Anton Hall, 1964.

Bleeker, C. J., ed. *Initiation*. Leiden: E. J. Brill, 1965.

Bödiger, Ute. *Die Religion der Tukano*. Cologne: Kölner Universitäts Verlag, 1965.

Böhme, Robert. *Orpheus: Der Sänger und seine Zeit*. Bern: Francke, 1970.

Bohannan, Laura. "A Genealogical Charter." *Africa* 22 (1952): 301–315.

137

Bohannan, Laura and Paul. *The Tiv of Central Nigeria.* London: International African Institute, 1953.

Bohannan, Paul. "Concepts of Time among the Tiv of Nigeria." *Southwestern Journal of Anthropology* 9 (1953): 251–262.

———. "Circumcision among the Tiv." *Man* 54 (1954): 2–6.

———. "A Tiv Political and Religious Idea." *Southwestern Journal of Anthropology* 11 (1955): 137–149.

———. "Beauty and Scarification among the Tiv." *Man* 56 (1956): 117–121.

Bohannan, Paul and Laura. *A Source Notebook in Tiv History and Social Organization.* New Haven: Human Relations Area Files, 1960.

Brandon, S. G. F. *History, Time, and Deity.* Manchester: Manchester University Press, 1965.

Brelich, Angelo. "The Historical Development of the Institution of Initiation in the Classical Age." *Acta Antiqua* 9 (1961): 267–283.

———. *Paides e Parthenoi.* Vol. 1. Rome: Ateneo, 1969.

———. "Symbol of a Symbol." In J. M. Kitagawa and C. H. Long, eds., *Myths and Symbols: Studies in Honor of Mircea Eliade.* Chicago: University of Chicago Press, 1969, pp. 201–206.

Brown, Judith K. "A Cross-Cultural Study of Female Initiation Rites." *American Anthropologist* 65 (1963): 837–853.

Bücheler, Franz, ed. *Berliner Klassikertexte.* Vol. 5, no. 1. Berlin: Weidmann, 1907.

Burkert, Walter. "Kekropidensage und Arrephoria: Vom Initiationsritus zum Panathenäenfest." *Hermes* 94 (1966): 1–25.

———. *Homo Necans.* Berlin: W. de Gruyter, 1972.

———. *Griechische Religion der archaischen und klassischen Epoche.* Stuttgart: W. Kohlhammer, 1977.

Butterworth, Edric Allan Schofield. *The Tree at the Navel of the Earth.* Berlin: W. de Gruyter, 1970.

Butterworth, G. W., ed. *Clement of Alexandria.* New York: G. P. Putnam, 1919.

Caillois, Roger. *L'Homme et le sacré.* Paris: Presses Universitaires de France, 1939.

Carnoy, A. *Dictionnaire étymologique des noms grecs des plantes.* Louvain: Publications Universitaires, 1959.

Cawte, E. C. *Ritual Animal Disguise.* Totowa, N.J.: Rowman and Littlefield, 1978.

Chirassi, Ileana. *Elementi di culture precereali nei miti e riti greci.* Rome: Ateneo, 1968.

Cohen, Yehudi A. *The Transition from Childhood to Adolescence.* Chicago: Aldine, 1964.

Cornford, F. M. "The *Aparkai* and the Eleusinian Mysteries." In *Essays and Studies Presented to William Ridgeway.* Cambridge: Cambridge University Press, 1913, pp. 153–166.

Curtis, Edward. *The North American Indian, Volume 1: Apache, Jicarillas, Navaho.* Cambridge, Mass.: Harvard University Press, 1907.

Dengler, H. "Das Haar-Ausreissen bei den Ticuna-Indianern West-Brasiliens." *Der Erdball* 1 (1926): 231–233.

Dieterich, Albrecht. *Eine Mithrasliturgie.* Leipzig: B. G. Teubner, 1903.

Downes, R. M. *The Tiv Tribe.* Kaduna: The Government Printer, 1933.

———. *Tiv Religion.* Ibadan: Ibadan University Press, 1971.

Driver, Harold E. "Girls' Puberty Rites in Western North America." *University of California Publications in Anthropological Records* 6 (1941): 21–90.

———. "Girls' Puberty Rites and Matrilocal Residence," *American Anthropologist* 71 (1969): 905–908.

———. "Reply to Opler on Apachean Subsistence, Residence, and Girls' Puberty Rites." *American Anthropologist* 74 (1972): 1147–51.

Dumont, Louis. "Les Mariages Nayar comme faits indiens." *L'Homme* 1 (1961): 11–36.

Dumont, P. E. *L'Agnihotra: Description de l'agnihotra dans le rituel védique.* Baltimore: Johns Hopkins University Press, 1939.

Durkheim, Emile. *The Elementary Forms of the Religious Life.* New York: Free Press, 1915.

Du Toit, Brian M. *Configurations of Cultural Continuity.* Rotterdam: A. A. Balkema, 1976.

East, Rupert, tr. and ed. *Akiga's Story: The Tiv Tribe as Seen by One of Its Members.* London: Oxford University Press, 1965.

Eliade, Mircea. *The Myth of the Eternal Return.* Princeton: Princeton University Press, 1954.

———. *Rites and Symbols of Initiation.* New York: Harper and Row, 1958.

———. *The Sacred and the Profane.* New York: Harcourt, Brace, 1959.

———. *Myths, Dreams, and Mysteries.* New York: Harper and Row, 1960.

———. *Shamanism: Archaic Techniques of Ecstasy.* Princeton: Princeton University Press, 1964.

———. *The Two and the One.* New York: Harper and Row, 1965.

———. *The Quest.* Chicago: University of Chicago Press, 1969.

———. *Histoire des croyances et des idées religieuses.* Vol. 1. Paris: Payot, 1976.

Engnell, Ivan. *Studies in Divine Kingship in the Ancient Near East.* Uppsala: Almquist and Wiksells, 1943.

Evans-Pritchard, E. E. *The Position of Women in Primitive Societies and Other Essays.* Oxford: Clarendon Press, 1966.

Farnell, Lewis Richard. *Cults of the Greek States.* 5 vols. Oxford: Clarendon Press, 1907.

Felice, Phillipe de. *L'Enchantement des danses et la magie du verbe.* Paris: A. Michel, 1957.

Fingarette, Herbert. *Confucius—The Secular as Sacred.* New York: Harper and Row, 1972.

Finley, Moses I. *The World of Odysseus.* New York: Viking, 1965.

Fock, Niels. *Waiwai: Religion and Society of an Amazonian Tribe.* Copenhagen: National Museum, 1963.

Fortes, Meyer. "Ritual and Office in Tribal Society." In Max Gluckman, ed., *Essays on the Ritual of Social Relations.* Manchester: University of Manchester Press, 1962, pp. 53–88.

Frazer, James George. *The Golden Bough.* 3rd ed., 12 vols. London: Macmillan, 1907–1912.

Freud, Sigmund. *Totem and Taboo.* New York: Vintage, 1918.

Frisbie, Charlotte Johnson. *Kinaaldá: A Study of the Navaho Girl's Puberty Ceremony.* Middletown: Wesleyan University Press, 1967.

Frisk, Hjalmar. *Griechisches etymologisches Wörterbuch.* 2 vols. Heidelberg: Carl Winter, 1973.

Gagé, Jean. *Matronalia.* Brussels: Collection Latomus, 1963.

Gasparini, E. "La danza circolare degli slavi." *Ricerche Slavistiche* 3 (1954): 72–89.

Gaster, Theodore. *Thespis*. New York: Harper and Row, 1961.

Gates, H. Phelps. *The Kinship Terminology of Homeric Greek*. Bloomington: Indiana University Press, 1971.

Gennep, Arnold van. *Mythes et légendes d'Australie*. Paris: E. Guilmoto, 1906.

———. *Desseins sur peaux d'opussum australiennes*. The Hague: Rijks Ethnographisch Museum, 1907.

———. *The Rites of Passage*. Chicago: University of Chicago Press, 1960.

Gernet, L., and A. Boulanger. *Le Génie grec dans la religion*. Paris: La Renaissance du Livre, 1932.

Gill, Sam D. "Prayer as Person: The Performative Force in Navajo Prayer Acts." *History of Religions* 17 (1977): 143–157.

Gillin, John. "Magical Fright." In W. Lessa and Evon Z. Vogt, eds., *Reader in Comparative Religion*. New York: Harper and Row, 1958, pp. 342–353.

Gimbutas, Marija. *The Gods and Goddesses of Old Europe*. Berkeley: University of California Press, 1974.

———. "The First Wave of Eurasian Steppe Pastoralists into Copper Age Europe." *Journal of Indo-European Studies* 5 (1977): 277–338.

Girardot, N. J. "Initiation and Meaning in the Tale of Snow White and the Seven Dwarfs." *Journal of American Folklore* 90 (1977): 274–300.

Gluckman, Max. "Les Rites de Passage." In Max Gluckman, ed., *Essays on the Ritual of Social Relations*. Manchester: University of Manchester Press, 1962, pp. 1–52.

Goffman, Erving. *Interaction Ritual: Essays in Face to Face Behavior*. Chicago: Aldine, 1967.

Goldman, Irving. *The Cubeo*. Urbana: University of Illinois Press, 1963.

———. "The Structure of Ritual in the Northwest Amazon." In Robert A. Manners, ed., *Process and Pattern in Culture: Essays in Honor of Julian H. Steward*. Chicago: Aldine, 1964, pp. 111–122.

Goodale, Jane. *Tiwi Wives*. Seattle: University of Washington Press, 1971.

Gough, E. Kathleen. "Female Initiation Rites on the Malabar Coast." *Journal of the Royal Anthropological Institute* 85 (1955): 45–80.

———. "The Nayars and the Definition of Marriage." *Journal of the Royal Anthropological Institute* 89 (1959): 23–24.

———. "Tiyyar: North Kerala." In David M. Schneider and Kathleen Gough, eds., *Matrilineal Kinship*. Berkeley: University of California Press, 1961, pp. 405–414.

Graf, F. *Eleusis und die orphische Dichtung Athens in vorhellenistischer Zeit*. Berlin: W. de Gruyter, 1974.

Granet, Marcel. *Danses et légendes de la Chine ancienne*. 2 vols. Paris: F. Alcan, 1926.

Greenberg, Joseph H. "The General Classification of Central and South American Languages." In A. F. C. Wallace, ed., *Men and Cultures*. Philadelphia: University of Pennsylvania Press, 1960, pp. 791–794.

Griaule, Marcel. *Conversations with Ogotêmmeli*. London: Oxford University Press, 1965.

Grinnell, George Bird. *The Cheyenne Indians*. Rpt. Lincoln: University of Nebraska Press, 1972.

Gronbech, Vilhelm. *Götter und Menschen: Griechische Geistesgeschichte*. Hamburg: Rowohlt, 1967.

Guthrie, W. K. C. *The Greeks and Their Gods*. Boston: Beacon, 1950.

Haekel, Josef. "Jugendweihe und Männerfest auf Feuerland." *Mitteilungen der Österreichischen Gesellschaft für Anthropologie* 73–77 (1947): 84–114.

Haile, Berard. "Navaho Chantways and Ceremonials." *American Anthropologist* 40 (1938): 539–552.

———. *Origin Legend of the Navaho Enemy Way*. New Haven: Yale University Press, 1938.

Hall, J. B., ed. *Claudian: De Raptu Proserpinae*. Cambridge: Cambridge University Press, 1969.

Hanke, Wanda. *Völkerkundliche Forschungen in Südamerika*. Braunschweig: Albert Lianbach, 1964.

Harding, M. Esther. "What Makes the Symbol Effective as a Healing Agent?" In Gerhard Adler, ed., *Current Trends in Analytical Psychology*. London: Tavistock, 1961, pp. 1–18.

Harrison, Jane Ellen. *Prolegomena to the Study of Greek Religion*. Cambridge: Cambridge University Press, 1903.

Hartmann, Günther. "Festa das Moças Novas (Tukuna/Westbrasilien)." *Baessler Archiv*, n.s. 15 (1967): 63–70.

Hayes, Rose Oldfield. "Female Genital Mutilation, Fertility Control, Women's Roles, and the Patrilineage in Modern Sudan: A Functional Analysis." *American Ethnologist* 2 (1975): 617–633.

Heestermann, J. C. *The Ancient Indian Royal Consecration*. The Hague: Mouton, 1957.

Henderson, Joseph L. *Thresholds of Initiation*. Middletown: Wesleyan University Press, 1967.

Hill, W. W. *The Agricultural and Hunting Methods of the Navaho Indians*. New Haven: Yale University Press, 1938.

Höfler, Otto. *Kultische Geheimbünde der Germanen*. Frankfurt: Moritz Diesterweg, 1934.

Holmberg (Harva), Uno. *Der Baum des Lebens*. Helsinki: Suomalainen Tiede Akatemia, 1922.

Hooke, S. H., ed. *Myth and Ritual*. London: Oxford University Press, 1933.

———, ed. *The Labyrinth*. New York: Macmillan, 1935.

———, ed. *Myth, Ritual, and Kingship*. Oxford: Clarendon Press, 1958.

Hubert, Henri, and Marcel Mauss. *Sacrifice: Its Nature and Function*. Chicago: University of Chicago Press, 1964.

Huizinga, Johan. *Homo Ludens*. Boston: Beacon Press, 1950.

Huxley, Julian, ed. "Ritualization of Behaviour in Animals and Man." *Philosophical Transactions of the Royal Society*, ser. B, 251 (1966).

Iyer, Anantha Krishna. *Lectures on Ethnography*. Calcutta: University of Calcutta, 1925.

James, E. O. *The Tree of Life*. Leiden: E. J. Brill, 1966.

Jeanmaire, Henri. *Couroi et Courètes*. Lille: Bibliothèque Universitaire, 1939.

Jensen, Adolf E. *Beschneidung und Reifezeremonien bei Naturvölker*. Stuttgart: Strecker und Schroeder, 1932.

———. *Myth and Cult among Primitive Peoples*. Chicago: University of Chicago Press, 1963.

Johansen, J. Prytz. "The Thesmophoria as a Women's Festival." *Temenos* 11 (1975): 78–87.

Kaberry, Phyllis M. *Aboriginal Woman: Sacred and Profane*. London: George Routledge, 1939.

Karsten, Rafael. *The Civilization of the South American Indians.* London: Kegan Paul, Trench and Trübner, 1926.

Keil, Charles. *Tiv Song.* Chicago: University of Chicago Press, 1979.

Keith, Anne. "The Navaho Girls' Puberty Ceremony." *El Palacio* 71 (1964): 27–36.

Kennedy, John G. "Circumcision and Excision in Egyptian Nubia." *Man* 5 (1970): 175–191.

Kerenyi, Caroly. "Persephone und Prometheus vom alter griechischer Mythen." In K. Hoppe, ed., *Hans Oppermann Festschrift,* in *Jahrbuch der Raabe Gesellschaft,* 1965, pp. 58–64.

———. "Voraussetzungen der Einweihung in Eleusis." In C. J. Bleeker, ed., *Initiation.* Leiden: E. J. Brill, 1965, pp. 59–64.

———. *Eleusis: Archetypal Image of Mother and Daughter.* New York: Pantheon, 1967.

Kern, Otto. *Die griechischen Mysterien der klassischen Zeit.* Berlin: Weidmann, 1927.

———, ed. *Orphicorum Fragmenta.* 2nd ed. Berlin: Weidmann, 1965.

Kiev, Ari, ed. *Magic, Faith, and Healing.* Glencoe: Free Press, 1964.

Klah, Hasteen. *Navajo Creation Myth: The Story of the Emergence.* Recorded by Mary C. Wheelwright. Santa Fe: Museum of Navajo Ceremonial Art, 1942.

Kloos, Peter. "Female initiation among the Maroni River Caribs." *American Anthropologist* 71 (1969): 898–905.

Kluckhohn, Clyde, and Dorothea Leighton. *The Navaho.* Garden City: Doubleday, 1962.

Knight, W. F. Jackson. *Cumaean Gates.* Oxford: Basil Blackwell, 1936.

Kramer, Samuel Noah. *The Sacred Marriage Rite.* Bloomington: Indiana University Press, 1969.

Kraus, T. *Hekate.* Heidelberg: Carl Winter, 1960.

Kunike, Hugo. "Der Fisch als Fruchtbarkeitssymbol bei den Waldindianern Südamerikas." *Anthropos* 7 (1912): 206–229.

La Fontaine, J. S. "Ritualization of Women's Life-Crises in Bugisu." In J. S. La Fontaine, ed., *The Interpretation of Ritual: Essays in Honour of A. I. Richards.* London: Tavistock, 1972, pp. 159–186.

Lanternari, Vittorio. *La Grande Festa.* Bari: Dedalo, 1976.

Leach, Edmund. "Ritualization in Man in Relation to Conceptual and Social Development." *Philosophical Transactions of the Royal Society,* ser. B, 251 (1966): 403–408.

———. "Ritual." In *International Encyclopedia of the Social Sciences.* Vol. 13. New York: Macmillan, 1968, pp. 520–526.

———. "A Critique of Yalman's Interpretation of Sinhalese Girl's Puberty Ceremonial." In Jean Pouillon and Pierre Maranda, ed., *Echanges et Communications: Mélanges offerts à Claude Lévi-Strauss.* The Hague: Mouton, 1970, pp. 819–828.

———. *Culture and Communication.* Cambridge: Cambridge University Press, 1976.

Leipoldt, Johannes. *Die Frau in der antiken Welt und im Urchristentums.* Gütersloh: Gerd Mohn, 1962.

Leeuw, Gerardius van. *In dem Himmel ist ein Tanz.* Munich: G. Ullmann, 1943.

Lévi-Strauss, Claude. *Structural Anthropology*. Garden City: Doubleday, 1963.
———. *The Raw and the Cooked*. New York: Harper and Row, 1969.
Lévy, Isidore. "Autour d'un roman mythologique égyptien." In *Mélanges Franz Cumont*. Brussels: Institut d'Histoire et de Philologie Orientales et Slaves, 1934, pp. 819–834.
Lienhardt, Godfrey. *Divinity and Experience: The Religion of the Dinka*. Oxford: Clarendon Press, 1961.
Lincoln, Bruce. "The Religious Significance of Women's Scarification among the Tiv." *Africa* 45 (1975): 316–326.
———. "Treatment of Hair and Fingernails among the Indo-Europeans." *History of Religions* 16 (1977): 351–362.
———. "Two Notes on Modern Rituals." *Journal of the American Academy of Religion* 45 (1977): 147–160.
———. "Women's Initiation among the Navaho: Myth, Rite, and Meaning." *Paideuma* 23 (1977): 255–263.
———. "The Rape of Persephone: A Greek Scenario of Women's Initiation." *Harvard Theological Review* 72 (1979): 223–235.
Lorenz, Konrad. "The Psychological Approach." In Julian Huxley, ed., "Ritualization of Behavior in Animals and Man." *Philosophical Transactions of the Royal Society*, ser. B, 251 (1966).
Maçoni, Vittorio. *L'iniziazione tribale*. Genoa: Tilgher, 1973.
Magnien, Victor. "Le Mariage chez les grecs." In *Mélanges Franz Cumont*. Brussels: Institut d'Histoire et de Philologie Orientales et Slaves, 1934, pp. 305–320.
Malten, L. "Altorphische Demetersagen." *Archiv für Religionswissenchaft* 12 (1909): 417–446.
Maringer, Johannes. *The Gods of Prehistoric Man*. London: Weidenfeld and Nichols, 1960.
Marrett, R. R. *The Threshold of Religion*. 2nd ed. London: Methuen, 1914.
Matthews, Washington. "The Night Chant." *Memoirs of the American Museum of Natural History* 6 (1902):
Mayer, Adrian C. *Land and Society in Malabar*. London: Oxford University Press, 1952.
McCartney, Eugene S. "How the Apple Became the Token of Love." *Transactions of the American Philosophical Association* 56 (1925): 70–81.
McCombe, Leonard, Evan Z. Vogt, and Clyde Kluckhohn. *Navaho Means People*. Cambridge, Mass.: Harvard University Press, 1951.
Meinardus, Otto. "Mythological, Historical, and Sociological Aspects of the Practice of Female Circumcision among the Egyptians." *Acta Ethnographica* 16 (1967): 387–397.
Métraux, Alfred. "Ritos de Transito de los Indios Sudamericanos. I: La Pubertad de las Mujeres." *Anales de arqueologia y etnologia* 6 (1945): 117–128.
———. *Religions et magies indiennes d'Amérique du Sud*. Paris: Gallimard, 1967.
Miner, Horace. "Body Ritual among the Nacirema." In William Lessa and Evon Z. Vogt, eds., *Reader in Comparative Religion*. New York: Harper and Row, 1972, pp. 414–418.
Modell, Judith. "Female Sexuality, Mockery, and a Challenge to Fate: A Reinterpretation of South Nayar Tālikettukalyānam," in Sherry Ortner and Harriet Whitehead, eds., *Sexual Meanings* (forthcoming).

Murphy, Robert and Yolanda. *Women of the Forest*. New York: Columbia University Press, 1974.

Mylonas, George. *Eleusis and the Eleusinian Mysteries*. Princeton: Princeton University Press, 1961.

Nair, P. T. "Tree Symbol Worship among Nairs of Kerala." In Sankar Sen Gupta, ed., *Tree Symbol Worship in India*. Calcutta: Indian Publication, 1965, pp. 98–100.

Nauck, Augustus, ed. *Tragicorum Graecorum Fragmenta*. Revised by Bruno Snell. Hildesheim: Georg Olms, 1964.

Neumann, Erich. *The Great Mother*. Princeton: Princeton University Press, 1963.

Newcomb, Franc Johnson, Stanley Fishler, and Mary C. Wheelwright. *A Study of Navajo Symbolism*. Papers of the Peabody Museum of Archaeology and Ethnology, vol 32. Copyright 1956 by the President and Fellows of Harvard College.

Nilsson, M. P. "Die eleusinischen Gottheiten." *Archiv für Religionswissenschaft* 32 (1935): 79–141.

———. *Greek Folk Religion*. New York: Harper and Row, 1961.

Nimuendaju, Curt. *The Tukuna*. Berkeley: University of California Press, 1952.

Oesterley, W. O. E. *The Sacred Dance*. Cambridge: Cambridge University Press, 1923.

O'Flaherty, Wendy Doniger. *Asceticism and Eroticism in the Mythology of Siva*. London: Oxford University Press, 1973.

———. *The Origin of Evil in Hindu Mythology*. Berkeley: University of California Press, 1976.

Oliveira, Roberto Cardosa de. "Totemismo Tukuna?" In *Beiträge zur Volkerkunde Südamerikas: Festgabe fur Herbert Baldus*. Hanover: Münstermann, 1964, pp. 231–248.

Opler, Morris E. "Cause and Effect in Apachean Agriculture, Division of Labor, Residence Patterns, and Girls' Puberty Rites." *American Anthropologist* 74 (1972): 1133–46.

Ortner, Sherry. "Is Female to Male as Nature Is to Culture?" In Michelle Zimbalist Rosaldo and Louise Lamphere, eds., *Woman, Culture, and Society*. Stanford: Stanford University Press, 1974, pp. 67–87.

Otten, Heinrich. *Hethitische Totenrituale*. Berlin: Akademie Verlag, 1958.

Ottenberg, Simon and Phoebe. *Cultures and Societies in Africa*. New York: Random House, 1960.

Otto, Walter. "The Meaning of the Eleusinian Mysteries." In Joseph Campbell, ed., *Papers from the Eranos Yearbooks, Volume 2: The Mysteries*. Princeton: Princeton University Press, 1955, pp. 14–31.

Pestalozza, Uberto. *L'Eternel féminin dans la religion méditerranéenne*. Brussels: Collection Latomus, 1965.

Picard, Charles. "L'Episode de Baubo dans les Mystères d'Eleusis." *Revue de l'Historie des Religions* 95 (1927): 220–255.

Piccaluga, G. "Ta Pherephattēs Anthologia." *Maia* 18 (1966): 232–253.

Pokorny, J. *Indogermanisches etymologisches Wörterbuch*. Bern: Francke, 1959.

Popp, V., ed. *Initiation: Zeremonien der Status änderung und des Rollenwechsels*. Frankfurt: Suhrkamp, 1969.

Preller, L. *Griechische Mythologie*. 4th ed. Berlin: Weidmann, 1894.

Pritchard, James B. *Ancient Near Eastern Texts*. 3rd ed. Princeton: Princeton University Press, 1969.

Bibliography

Puntoni, Vittorio. *L'Inno Omerico a Demetra*. Livorno: R. Giusti, 1896.

Queiróz, Mauricio Vinhas de. " 'Cargo cult'na amazônia: Observações sôbre o milenarismo Tukuna." *América Latina* 6/4 (Oct.–Dec. 1963): 43–61.

Radcliffe-Brown, A. R. *Structure and Function in Primitive Society*. Glencoe: Free Press, 1952.

———. *The Andaman Islanders*. Glencoe: Free Press, 1964.

Radin, Paul. *Indians of South America*. Garden City: Doubleday, Doran, 1942.

Rao, M. S. A. *Social Change in Malabar*. Bombay: Popular Press, 1957.

Rappaport, Roy A. *Pigs for the Ancestors*. New Haven: Yale University Press, 1968.

Reichard, Gladys. *Social Life of the Navajo Indians*. New York: Columbia University Press, 1928.

———. *Prayer: The Compulsive Word*. Seattle: University of Washington Press, 1944.

———. *Navaho Religion: A Study of Symbolism*. 2nd ed. Princeton: Princeton University Press, 1974.

Reichel-Dolmatoff, Gerardo. *Amazonian Cosmos: The Sexual and Religious Symbolism of the Tukano Indians*. Chicago: University of Chicago Press, 1971.

Reik, Theodor. *Ritual: Psychoanalytic Studies*. London: Hogarth Press, 1931.

———. *The Creation of Woman*. New York: George Braziller, 1960.

———. *The Temptation*. New York: George Braziller, 1961.

Reminick, Ronald A. "The Symbolic Significance of Ceremonial Defloration among the Amhara of Ethiopia." *American Ethnologist* 3 (1976): 751–763.

Richards, Audrey I. *Chisungu: A Girls' Initiation Ceremony among the Bemba of Northern Rhodesia*. London: Faber and Faber, 1956.

Richardson, N. J. *The Homeric Hymn to Demeter*. Oxford: Clarendon Press, 1964.

Richter, Gisela M. A. *Red-Figured Athenian Vases in the Metropolitan Museum of Art*. 2 vols. New Haven: Yale University Press, 1936.

Rigby, Peter. "The Structural Context of Girls' Puberty Rites." *Man* 2 (1970): 434–444.

Ross, John Alan. "The Puberty Ceremony of the Chimbu Girl." *Anthropos* 60 (1965): 423–432.

Rowe, Charles F. "Abdominal Cicatrisations of the Munshi Tribe, Nigeria." *Man* 28 (1928): 179–180.

Sahlins, Marshall D. "The Segmentary Lineage: An Organization of Predatory Expansion." *American Anthropologist* 63 (1961): 322–345.

Scarpi, Paolo. *Letture sulla religione classica: L'Inno Omerico a Demetra*. Florence: Leo Olschke, 1976.

Schaden, Egon. *Ensaio etno-sociológico sôbre a mitologia heróica de algumas tribos indígenas do Brasil*. São Paulo: Universidade de São Paulo, 1946.

Schechner, Richard, and Mady Schuman, eds. *Ritual, Play, and Performance*. New York: Seabury Press, 1976.

Schlegel, Alice. "The Adolescent Socialization of the Hopi Girl." *Ethnology* 12 (1973): 449–462.

Schultz, Harold. "Tukuna Maidens Come of Age." *National Geographic* 116 (1959): 628–649.

———. "Fra i Tucuna dell' alta Amazzonia." *Atlante* 1 (1961): 121–153.

Skov, G. E. "The Priestess of Demeter and Kore and Her Role in the Initiation of Women at the Festival of the Haloa at Eleusis." *Temenos* 11 (1975): 136–147.

Smith, W. Robertson. *Lectures on the Religion of the Semites.* London: A. and C. Black, 1894.

Snell, Bruno, ed. *Pindarus.* Leipzig: B. G. Teubner, 1964.

Speiser, Felix. "Die eleusinischen Mysterien als primitive Initiation." *Zeitschrift für Ethnologie* 60 (1928): 362–372.

————. "Über Initiationen in Australien und Neuguinea." *Verhandlungen der naturforschenden Gesellschaft in Basel* (1929): 56–258.

Spencer, Katherine. *Reflections of Social Life in the Navaho Origin Myth.* Albuquerque: University of New Mexico Press, 1947.

Tastevin, C. "Le Poisson symbole de fécondité ou de fertilité chez les Indiens de l'Amérique du Sud." *Anthropos* 9 (1914): 405–417.

Thurnwald, Richard. "Primitive Initiations- und Wiedergeburtsriten." *Eranos Jahrbuch* 7 (1939): 321–398.

Thurston, Edgar. *Ethnographic Notes in Southern India.* Madras: Government Press, 1906.

————, and K. Rangachari. *Castes and Tribes of Southern India.* 7 vols. Madras: Government Press, 1909.

Turner, Victor. *The Forest of Symbols.* Ithaca: Cornell University Press, 1967.

————. *The Drums of Affliction.* Oxford: Clarendon Press, 1968.

————. *The Ritual Process.* Chicago: Aldine, 1969.

Turner, Victor and Edith. *Image and Pilgrimage in Christian Culture: Anthropological Perspectives.* New York: Columbia University Press, 1978.

Vernant, Jean. "Le Mariage en Grèce archaïque." *La parola del passato* 148 (1973): 51–74.

Visca, D. "Le iniziazioni feminili: Un problema da riconsiderare." *Religioni e Civiltà* 2 (1976): 241–274.

Vogliano, Achille, ed. *Papiri dell'Università degli Studi de Milano.* Vol. 1. Milan: Ulrico Hoepli, 1937.

Vorman, P. "Initiationsfeiern der Jünglinge und Mädchen bei den Monumbo-Papua." *Anthropos* 10 (1915): 159–179.

Wedgewood, Camilla H. "Girls' Puberty Rites in Manam Island, New Guinea." *Oceania* 4 (1933): 132–155.

Weiser, Lily. *Altgermanische Jünglingsweihe und Männerbünde.* Baden: Konkordia A.-G., 1927.

West, M. L., ed. *Hesiod: Theogony.* Oxford: Clarendon Press, 1966.

Wendel, Carol, ed. *Scholia in Theocritum Vetera.* Stuttgart: B. G. Teubner, 1967.

Wheelwright, Mary C. *Emergence Myth According to the Hanelthnayhe or Upward-Reaching Rite.* Recorded by Berard Haile. Santa Fe: Museum of Navajo Ceremonial Art, 1949.

Whiteman, J. "Girls' Puberty Ceremonies among the Chimbu." *Anthropos* 60 (1965): 410–422.

Whiting, John W. M., Richard Kluckhohn, and Albert Anthony. "The Function of Male Initiation Ceremonies at Puberty." In Eleanor E. Maccoby, et al., eds., *Readings in Social Psychology.* New York: Holt, Rinehart and Winston, 1958, pp. 359–370.

Widengren, Geo. *The King and the Tree of Life in Ancient Near Eastern Religion.* Uppsala: A. B. Lundquist, 1951.

————. "Le Symbolisme de la ceinture." *Iranica Antiqua* 8 (1969): 133–155.

Wikander, Stig. *Der arische Männerbund.* Lund: Gleerupska Universitets Bokhandeln, 1938.

Wilamowitz-Moellendorff, Ulrich von. *Der Glaube der Hellenen.* 2 vols. Berlin: Weidmann, 1932.

Willoughby, Harold R. *Pagan Regeneration.* Chicago: University of Chicago Press, 1929.

Witherspoon, Gary. *Language and Art in the Navajo Universe.* Ann Arbor: University of Michigan Press, 1977.

Wolfram, Richard. "Sword Dances and Secret Societies." *Journal of the English Folk Dance and Song Society* 1 (1932): 34–41.

———. "Weiberbunde." *Zeitschrift für Volkskunde* 42 (1932): 137–142.

Wyman, Leland C. *Blessingway.* Recorded and translated by Berard Haile. Tucson: University of Arizona Press, 1970.

Wyman, Leland, and Flora Bailey. "Navajo Girl's Puberty Rite." *New Mexico Anthropologist* 25 (1943): 3–12.

Wyman, Leland, and Clyde Kluckhohn. "Navaho Classification of Their Song Ceremonials." *Memoirs of the American Anthropological Association* 50 (1938): 3–38.

Yalman, Nur. "On the Purity of Women in the Castes of Ceylon and Malabar." *Journal of the Royal Anthropological Institute* 93 (1963): 25–58.

Young, Frank W. *Initiation Ceremonies: A Cross-Cultural Study of Status Dramatization.* Indianapolis: Bobbs-Merrill, 1965.

Zeller, Moritz. *Die Knabenweihen: Ein psychologisch-ethnologische Studie.* Bern: P. Haupt, 1923.

Zerries, Otto. *Wild- und Buschgeister in Südamerika.* Wiesbaden: Franz Steiner, 1954.

———. "Die Tanzmasken der Tukuna- und Juri-Taboca-Indianer." *Paideuma* 7 (1961): 362–376.

———. "Primitive South America and the West Indies." In Walter Krickeberg, et al., *Pre-Columbian American Religion.* New York: Holt, Rinehart and Winston, 1968, pp. 230–316.

———. "Die Bedeutung des Federschmuckes des Südamerikanischen Schamanen und dessen Beziehung zur Vogelwelt." *Paideuma* 23 (1977): 277–324.

Zuntz, Günther. *Persephone.* Oxford: Clarendon Press, 1971.

Index